Camping Your Way Through Europe

The Dream Trip You Thought You Couldn't Afford

by Carol Mickelsen

Illustrations by Jack Tavenner

Every effort to has been made to make this book as accurate as possible, but information for travelers can change quickly. The author and publisher accept no responsibility for any inconvenience, disappointment, or injury resulting from information contained in *Camping Your Way Through Europe*.

Published by: Affordable Travel Press
P.O. Box 3296
Half Moon Bay, CA 94019
USA
415-726-4777

First Printing, July 1996

Library of Congress Catalog Number

Mickelsen, Carol

Camping Your Way through Europe/Carol Mickelsen

1. Travel/Budget/Europe   2. Camping/Europe
3. Driving/Europe   4. Cooking/Camping

ISBN 0-9652421-0-2

Illustrations and maps: Jack Tavenner
Cover design: Donna Davis
Interior design: Fog Press
Production: Fog Press
Index: Joan Dickey
Printing: Griffin Printing

Dedicated to my parents, Pat and Lu Patterson, who taught me to be forever optimistic, believe in myself, and to love life.

Contents

Introduction   1

Reasons People Give for Not Camping Abroad   4

Planning   7

Your Itinerary   7

3–4 Months Before Departure   8

    Purchasing Your Airline Ticket   8

    Get your Documents   9

    Getting Vehicle Information   9

2–3 Months Before Departure   11

3–4 Weeks Before Departure   12

How to Pack   13

Camping Equipment List   15

1 Week Before Departure   18

On the Road   18

    Arrival at Departure Airport   18

    Arrival at Destination Airport with Bikes   19

Picking Up Your Vehicle   20

The Navigator's Job   22

Camping and Cooking   27

Finding the Camping Place   27
Grocery Shopping   29
Setting Up A Tent Camp   31
Camp Cooking Hints   32

Camping Recipes   37

Cooking Definitions   46

Countries to Visit   49

Austria   49
  Salzburg   50
  Salzkammerg Ut Region   51
  Lechtaler Alps   53
Czech and Slovak Republics   59
  Bohemia   60
  Moravia   63
  Slovakia   63
Denmark   69
  Zealand   70
  Funen   73
  Jutland   74
France   79
  Paris   81
  Loire Valley   83
  Burgundy and Rhone Valley Area   85
  French Alps   86
  Provence   87
  Cote d'Azur   88
  Bordeaux Region   89
  Basque Country   90
  Gascogne   91
  Alsace-Lorraine   91
  Normandy   92
  Britagne   93
Germany   99
  Bavaria   100
  Bavarian Alps   101
  Bavarian Forest (Bayerischer Wald)   102
  Baden-Württemberg   102
  Black Forest (Schwarzwald)   103
  Lake Constance (Bodensee)   103

    Danube River Area   103
    Rhineland   104

Greece   109
    Athens   110
    Delphi   111
    Peloponnese   111
    The Island of Crete   113
    The Island of Rhodes   114
    The Island of Tilos   114
    The Island of Kos   115
    The Island of Patmos   115
    The Island of Samothrace   115
    The Island of Corfu   115
    The Island of Zakynthos   116
    The Island of Skiathos   116
    The Island of Mykonos   116
    The Island of Paros   116
    The Island of Folegandros   117
    The Island of Thira (Santorini)   117

Hungary   121
    Budapest   122
    Danube Bend Area   123
    Western Trandanubia   124
    Balaton Lake   124
    Southern Transdanubia   125
    Great Plain Puszta   126
    Northern Hungary   127

Italy   131
    Rome   132
    Umbria   133
    Tuscany   136
    Marche   138
    Gran Sasso   139
    Amalfi Coast   140
    Northern Italy   140
    Valle D'Aosta   141
    Dolomites and South Tyrol   142
    Venice and the Veneto   143
    The Lakes Area   144

Netherlands   149
    Amsterdam   149
    Haarlem   150

Leiden   151
The Hague   151
Hoge Veluwe   151

Norway   155
  Oslo   157
  Lillehammer   159
  Bergen   160
  Aurlandsfjord and Flam   161
  Jostedalspreen Glacier   161
  Geirangerfjord   161
  Romsdalsfjord and Trollveggen   162

Poland   167
  Warsaw   167
  Zakopane   168
  Krakow   169
  Czestochowa   170
  Zamosc   170
  Pomerania   170

Portugal   175
  Lisbon   176
  Just North of Lisbon   177
  Just West of Lisbon   177
  Southern Coast of Portugal/The Algarve   178
  Central Portugal   178
  North Along the Atlantic Coast   179
  Northern Portugal   180
  North of Oporto on the Coast   180
  Close to the Northern Spanish Border   181

Spain   185
  Madrid   186
  El Escorial   187
  Salamanca   187
  Segovia   188
  Toledo   189
  Barcelona   189
  Montserrat   190
  Tarragonia   190
  Costa Brava   191
  Baleraric Islands Area   192
  Andulusia   193
  Basque Country   194

Sweden   199
  Stockholm   200
  Uppsala   201
  Gothenburg   202
  Bohuslan   203
  Malmo   203
  Lund   204
  Lake Siljan Area   204
  Visby Island   205
  Vadstena   205

Switzerland   209
  Berne   210
  Interlaken   211
  Jungfrau Region   211
  The Lake Region   212
  Ticino—The Italian Switzerland   212
  Graubunden   214
  Engadine Valley   214
  Bodensee Area   215
  Central Switzerland   216
  Swiss Jura   217

Western Turkey   221
  Istanbul   223
  Bursa   225
  Canakkale   225
  Ayvalik   226
  Foca   227
  Ismir   227
  Ephesus   227
  Pamukkale   228
  Bodrum   228
  Western Mediterranean Coast   229

Appendix   233
  Using Public Transportation   233
  Tourist Offices   233
  Food Markets   233
  Buying Gas   234
  Parking   234
  Road Signs   234
  Border Crossing   234
  Avoiding Burglary from Your Vehicle   235
  Vehicle Insurance   235

Renting Your Vehicle   236
International Vehicle Rental Companies   236
International Camper Van Rental Companies   237
Document Information   238
Visa   238
International Driving Permit (IDP)   238
International Student Identity Card (ISIC)   238
Federal International Youth Travel Organization Card (FIYTO)   238
Senior Citizen Card   239
International Camping Carnet Card   239
Resources   239
Recommended General Budget Guide Books   239
Camping Equipment   239

Index   245

About the Author   264
About the Illustrator   264

Introduction

I've done it and
you can too!

If you've always wanted to travel in Europe but don't think you can afford it, this book is for you. After years of travel and practice, I've discovered practical tips for saving not only money but precious travel time and frustration. I'll take you through the steps of renting your vehicle, driving and navigating through foreign countries where you don't speak the language, shopping for fresh local food, and cooking delicious dinners. I also provide the basics for camper van camping and detailed instructions on tent camping with a car.

I'm happy when I'm camping. For me there's nothing like sitting by a pleasant creek, listening to the gurgling water, watching the birds and clouds, enjoying a good book, and relishing an idyllic setting that I could not possibly afford in a hotel.

After setting up the cooking area in the late afternoon, my companion and I pour ourselves a glass of local wine, arrange the fresh and inviting food we bought at the open market that morning, and then begin to prepare our meal. We laugh and talk. The meal is satisfying, and we have enjoyed it in lovely surroundings, without hunting for a restaurant or paying a big tab. We feel wonderful.

I always bring my bike. Riding my bike through towns and countryside allows me to wander where whim takes me. The fresh air is kissing my face, I smile at locals, savor the sights, and get exercise. You see so much more than you would in a car or walking. You'll find tips for how to travel with your bike.

When I spend the last night of a trip in a hotel, before catching my flight to return home, I always miss my little home out in the country. I miss the fresh air, hearing the birds singing, and having my camp-made cup of coffee or tea in the morning.

I can travel a great deal because I do it so inexpensively. Let me show you how you can too!

Cost of trip   I've traveled with a companion in Central and Northern Europe (the most expensive countries) for 70 to 98 dollars per day, in Eastern Europe for 35 to 60 dollars a day; and in Greece and Turkey for 51 to 85 dollars a day. This amount is for two persons traveling together in 1994–1995 and includes camping fees, gas, food, beer or wine for dinner, a beer or cappuccino in a cafe in the afternoon or evening, and sightseeing fees. It doesn't include eating in restaurants, airfare or vehicle rental costs.

Expense Expectations

For Two Persons *If Guidelines in Book Are Followed*

	North & Central Europe	Turkey & Greece	Eastern Europe
GAS maximum 150 miles per day	$12–25	$10–25	$10–25
GROCERIES/ DINNER main dish, starch, vegetable, bread	$10–12	$6–8	$5–6
BOTTLE OF WINE	$7–8	$5–6	$3–4
GROCERIES/ BREAKFAST cereal, bread, coffee/tea	$3–4	$2–3	$2–3
GROCERIES/ LUNCH make sandwich, fruit, soda	$3–4	$2–3	$2–3
TREAT sitting in a cafe	$8–10	$6–7	$3–4
CAMPING PLACE FEE (not upscale)	$18–20	$10–18	$5–7
MUSEUM/ HISTORIC SITE FEE	$10–15	$10–15	$5–8
LAUNDRY	No extra cost; done at the campsite and dried in vehicle while traveling		
TOTAL FOR TWO PERSONS (less vehicle rental†)	$71–98	$51–85	$35–60

†See chart "Average Weekly Rental Rates" in Appendix and divide that amount in half for per-person cost.

Reasons People Give for Not Camping Abroad

I can't cook.	I will teach you how to have absolutely delicious meals that are easy and fun to prepare. I provide detailed instructions so that even if you never cook at home, you can master the few techniques that make prepping, cooking, and cleaning up after a meal easy. I predict these will be satisfying meals, and you won't often feel the need to go out.
I don't know what to rent.	Tent camping is less expensive than camper van camping, because the vehicle and the camp fees are less. I prefer tent camping to camper van camping when I am traveling in countries where it is warm, because I prefer being outdoors. I want a camper van when I am traveling in a country where it rains a lot or where the evenings are cool. Then the extra expense seems worthwhile.
I don't own camping equipment.	If you want to try tent camping but don't have any equipment, you will have some extra expense on your first trip. But camping equipment lasts for many years. It's a good investment. The items I recommend purchasing will cost only the equivalent of two or three days' worth of hotels and restaurants.
It requires too much luggage.	Taking it all with you on the plane isn't difficult. All the equipment needed for tent camping can fit into four duffels with room left over, and everything is checked. Use a large carry-on bag for your clothing and personal items.
	I always take our bikes because I enjoy using them to get around the towns, villages, and countryside. If you are camper van camping, you will have room to take bikes without any additional luggage cost. If you are tent camping, you'll need the four pieces of allowed luggage for camping equipment. Your bikes will be charged as additional luggage.
Driving in a foreign country is too difficult.	Driving in a foreign country and finding your way to a campsite takes teamwork. I'll show you how a good navigator can ensure a smooth and relaxing trip.

I don't speak a foreign language.

Traveling in the countryside, where few people speak English, might seem difficult. I have included fill-in forms of often-asked questions in the language of each country. Use them to ask local people how to get where you want to go.

I don't know where to go.

Each country's sightseeing highlights are described so that you can plan a relaxing itinerary and avoid excessive driving.

Camping places close to the main sights are listed, along with directions on how to reach them. General information is included about camping and grocery shopping in each country.

I might be burglarized.

Burglary is not usually a problem in camping places. They are generally safe. But I will tell you how to avoid being burglarized while you are parked in a tourist area.

Planning

Your Itinerary

Where you go is often determined by when you go. Here are some important considerations.

Weather

When you are tent camping, weather is an important factor. When you have an camper van, it is less so. Electricity is available, so with an camper van you can camp even during the colder, rainier months. Rural camping places are often open only from the end of April through mid-October. Camping places closer to cities are usually open all year. (See Appendix: "Temperature and Rainfall.")

Costs

If you do your own cooking, you can keep your costs down. Groceries in Central and Northern Europe are more expensive than in Eastern Europe but are still reasonable if you buy fresh vegetables and less expensive cuts of meat and fish and shop often in open markets. Vehicle cost varies considerably, depending on the type of vehicle you rent and the country in which you rent.

Destination

What do you want to see and experience? If you love flowers, you'll find late April and May to be spectacular in the Netherlands. If you want to visit the major historical sights in Greece or Italy, ideal times are late April through June and September through early October because you'll avoid crowds and heat. For Central and Eastern Europe, go in May through early October. Keep in mind that July and August are the hottest months in

Europe and the time when Europeans vacation. When possible, avoid beaches, lakes, and major sights during these months. Eastern Europe and Scandinavia are wonderful during these summer months.

Duration

If you are renting a vehicle, you may need to return it to the same location you picked it up. Design a flexible itinerary that allows you to begin your trip one way and return a different way. You will want to be able to make changes when you actually get on the road and start camping. It's a good idea never to travel more than two hundred miles in one day. If you need to travel that far in one day, plan some easier days around it. Keep in mind it will take you two to three times longer to get anywhere on small country roads than on autostratas.

3–4 Months Before Departure

Purchasing Your Airline Ticket

Lowest airfares

Your travel agent is critical here. You need someone who is willing to search for the least expensive airfare, a feat that requires extra work on the agent's part. Airlines offer bargain fares when they think a particular flight might not fill. Your agent should check the computer for these before you purchase your ticket. Reduced fare tickets are also often available during the off-season. However, once you buy a bargain ticket, you usually can't get a refund.

Number of stops

Ask how many stops your flight makes before it reaches your destination. Each time you stop, there is a chance for delay. The most desirable flight goes nonstop to your destination.

Seat assignment   When you purchase your ticket, request your seat assignment for both legs of your trip. Decide when you make your reservation whether you want the smoking or nonsmoking section, and the aisle, middle, or window seat. Reconfirm your seat assignment one month before departure, because the type of plane scheduled can change.

Examine ticket carefully   Immediately upon receiving your ticket, examine it carefully for mistakes. It is your responsibility to make the final check, not the travel agent's. Mark your departure time on your calendar. Memorize it several days before departure so you don't make a last-minute mistake. Understand your arrival time at your destination. Going to Europe, you'll probably arrive a calendar day later than you started.

Get your Documents

Apply for any documents you will need or qualify for: passport, visa, international driving permit, senior citizen card, international student identity card, federal international youth travel organization card, and camping carnet card. (See Appendix: "Documents").

Getting Vehicle Information

Get vehicle information early   Begin requesting information from both the large rental companies and the independents. (See Appendix: "International Vehicle Rental Companies").

Determine whether or not it is cheaper to make this reservation yourself, than have your travel agent make it. He or she may be able to do it at no additional cost to you. Smaller independents might be less expensive if you make a reservation directly with them.

Determine which vehicle fits your needs

When choosing the type of vehicle to rent, keep in mind its ease of handling on small country roads, winding hillsides, and narrow streets in historic town centers. Don't forget you'll also have to park it. Then decide how much living room you need to be comfortable. Consider the cost of the type of fuel it needs. It's best to choose the smallest camper van that you can be comfortable in. Unless you plan to spend most of your time on autostratas, you'll find the wider and longer camper vans awkward, tiring, and nerve-wracking to drive in the old centers of towns and cities in Europe.

Pick up and return

Find out where and when you will pick up and drop off the vehicle. Talk about number of days, rather than weeks, when discussing length of use. Document the cost of early and late returns.

Reserve as soon as possible

After you've shopped around and made a decision, book the vehicle as soon as possible. This is particularly important with camper vans. Companies don't keep many camper vans in inventory. Some companies also have sleeping bags, camp chairs, and bike racks that can be rented. If you rent these, be sure to get documentation on your reservation.

2–3 Months Before Departure

Renting your vehicle

Vehicle costs vary considerably from country to country, depending on the VAT (value added tax, around 20–28%) and the competition. (See Appendix: "Average Weekly Auto Rental Rates").

There is a sizable cost for insurance, and you'll need more than just basic insurance. (See Appendix: "Vehicle Insurance").

If you use an insurance company other than the rental company's for your supplemental insurance, be sure to carry with you well-documented proof of this insurance. Also get documented proof that the rental company will honor this insurance and won't require you to purchase more. Have the company document any deposits that are required and how they must be made. Don't assume you can use your charge card for security deposits.

If you are renting a car, trunk size is important. You'll probably need a mid-size vehicle to get all your gear in the trunk. On the spot you can sometimes get an upgrade from an economy-size car for no extra charge, since smaller cars are more in demand and rental agencies sometimes run out. Don't pay extra charges if the type of vehicle you ordered is not available and a larger, more expensive car is substituted. Remember to consider how fuel-efficient the vehicle is.

Travel guides and maps

Buy travel guides and maps now and start using them to plan your trip. (See Appendix: "Resources," Recommended General Budget Guide Books and Maps).

I also always take a phrase book in the local language, language tapes, a language dictionary, plus photocopies of "fill-in" directional sheets for each country. (See sections at the end of each country.)

Detailed maps are vital	Purchase detailed maps before you go so you don't have to spend valuable time shopping for them after you arrive. The Michelin series is excellent. Check the index on the map to see if there is a symbol for camping places (usually it's a tent). Before you purchase a map, find on it several camping places listed in this book. It's fun and reassuring to locate some of the camping places you'll stay in before you leave. Buy a map for each area you'll be traveling in. You'll need at least an expansion of 1/400,000 or 1 cm: 4 km in order to get to your campsite easily.

Determine the location of the pick up and return of the vehicle and what hours the facility is open. Is there a free shuttle to this location, either from the airport or from your hotel? Consider spending the first night in a hotel to recover from jet lag and arrange for vehicle pickup on the day after your arrival in Europe. If you have an early flight for your return home, it might also be wise to spend the last night in a hotel and arrange to return your vehicle the day before your flight home. Select a hotel from your guide book and make reservations; by fax is easiest.

Get price quotes from several companies listed in the Appendix. You will probably save money by booking and paying in the United States.

Photocopy all important documents	Have everything documented on your vehicle reservation voucher, including the reservation number. Make a photocopy of your vehicle reservation, your airline tickets, and your passport.

Get written directions from arrival airport to pickup site	Get very specific written directions from the rental office concerning your pickup of the vehicle. Camper van rental locations are often in a suburb outside the main city center, and the taxi driver will need help with directions.

3–4 Weeks Before Departure

Pack carry-ons and duffels	Though it might seem too early, packing your bags now allows time for you to purchase things you still need. You are calmer now than you will be later. Make piles of things you are going to pack. Make a list of the items you will put in just before leaving and place it with your baggage. Early packing frees your mind.

Type and amount of baggage

Airlines allow two pieces of baggage per person to be checked in. Be sure yours is collapsible. When traveling in your camper van or car, you won't have room to store hard-sided baggage.

How to Pack

Packing a bike

Take a bike rack if you are not able to arrange for one through the car rental company. A bike rack can be partially disassembled and strapped to one of the duffels. I have purchased hard-sided bike boxes for the plane and have always been able to store them at the camper van pickup site. When I rent a car, I place them in long-term storage at the train station. Cardboard boxes are sometimes available at bike stores and airlines for a very reasonable price. If you plan to use an airline box, reconfirm that they are available, reserve them, and find out where you pick them up. *Arrive at the airport 3 to 4 hours ahead of departure so that you can pack your bike in an out-of-the-way place at the airport.* The advantage of this method is that you don't have the problem of storing a hard-sided bike box. The cardboard boxes can be discarded at your destination and the bought new for the return home. The disadvantage is that the airlines refuse any liablity and may ask you to sign a waiver.

Packing a tent

When you are tent camping from a car, allocate one and a half duffels for the "bedroom," meaning the tent, sleeping mats, inflatable pillows, and sleeping bags.

The second duffel is for the "kitchen," meaning the camping tarp, pots and pans, cooking utensils, and so on. Fuel for the stove won't be allowed on the airplane, so consider buying a stove when you arrive. Then you'll also be sure about the gas fitting and the availability of the gas the stove uses.

The third duffel is the "living room," meaning a camping tarp, collapsible ground chairs, tape recorder, guide books, maps, and candleholder or light. That adds up to three and a half duffels, so you will still have extra room. (See "Camping Equipment").

Packing personal items

All personal items must fit into one carry-on bag per person. Consider weight and possible wrinkling when choosing what to bring. The relief of not having to tote heavy baggage, and of not having to store unneeded items during your trip, makes this trimming step worthwhile.

- Bring two outfits of casual clothes for cool weather and two for warm weather. Also bring two outfits for sightseeing and one warm and comfy outfit to wear around camp.
- Bring shoes appropriate for walking, biking, and hiking, as well as for around camp.
- Bring a lightweight bag to carry your toiletries into the shower. Include lightweight bath towels that can dry in the vehicle as you drive.
- Bring quick-drying nylon underwear.
- Earplugs come in handy to block out camping place noise if you go to bed early.
- Photocopies of "Asking for Directions" forms

Camping Equipment List

Stove

Airlines won't let you pack fuel for a stove, and the camp stove you already own might not use the fuel that is readily available in the area you'll be traveling. So my first purchase on arrival is a camp stove. They are found in a hardware store, sporting goods store, or camping place store, and will have the gas fitting size of the propane available.

Stove board

Positioning your stove on a flat surface is critical to successful cooking. The ground isn't always level. You can make a "stove board" by measuring the bottom of the kitchen duffel. Use this measurement to cut $\frac{1}{4}$-inch plywood into the same shape. Cover it with contact paper. Place this stove board on the bottom of your kitchen duffel and pack things on top of it.

Pot and pan	You need only one pot and one pan, but it is critical that they are the right ones.

- Sauté pan:
  8-inch heavy aluminum or Calphalon
  1-quart size with sloping sides and lid (preferably a rounded lid). Lightweight, straight-sided camping pans won't work with my recipes.
- Pot:
  1-½ quart with lid. This can be lightweight.

Knives	Bring two sharp knives of good quality: an 8-inch and a 4-inch. Don't frustrate yourself with dull or poor-quality knives.

More vital cooking tools	One 8-inch and two 4-inch bowls

12-inch metal tongs
Matches
Flashlight
Headlight (found at camping stores; great for twilight)
Squeeze-dry kitchen cloths (found at camping stores)
Sponge
Pot scrubber
Two cutting boards
Can opener
Wine bottle opener
Bottle opener
Small jar for mixing salad dressing
1 quart storage container
Plastic plates, cups, and bowls
Eating utensils
Your favorite dried spices

(Many of these can be purchased after you arrive, but then you have the trouble of finding where to buy them.)

Sleeping equipment	Tent

Sleeping bags
Inflatable pillows, pillowcases
Inflatable sleeping mats

Biking accessories	Helmets

Lock
Repair kit

Relaxing at the campsite

Collapsible ground chairs
Two camping tarps (one for the "kitchen" and one for the "living room")
Books
Tape recorder and tapes
Candleholder and candles
Battery-operated mini-lights

Keeping clean

- Plastic shower bag (Use to warm water during the day on your dashboard or back window shelf. Then use as a shower in camping places that don't have hot water, or hang to use in your kitchen.)
- Basin or large bowl (for washing vegetables and dishes as you cook)

1 Week Before Departure

Pack purse, carry-on, and belt bag

Yes, pack your purse, carry-on, and belt bag now. The day before and the day of departure are hectic enough without having this to do. Include: money, airline tickets, passport, vehicle voucher, traveler's checks, some money in the currency of your arrival country (to avoid standing in line upon arrival to change money), credit cards, driver's license, international driver's license and camping carnet card, and insurance papers. (See Appendix: "Documents").

Gather airplane comfort items

You might want to include: an inflatable neck pillow, eye shades, earplugs, medicines, a book, a toothbrush, toilet articles, sunglasses, and prescription glasses. I always include language tapes and a small tape player.

On the Road

Arrival at Departure Airport

If with bikes

Allow extra time if you are bringing bikes. They are bulky and can cause frustration, but they are worth the effort. If you are using airline cardboard boxes, *arrive at the airport 3–4 hours before departure.* Have one person stay in an out-of-the-way place with bikes, bike rack, and baggage. The other person picks up the bike boxes and two carts. Dismantle and pack bikes and bike rack. *Be sure to have easy to find notes on how to reassemble and repack them.* Bring duct tape for bike boxes and straps for the bike rack. If you have hard sized bike boxes, have one person stay with the baggage while the other gets two carts. Then one person stays with the baggage and stands in line for check-in while the other takes the bikes to the oversize luggage area.

Get on plane early

I like to get on the airplane as soon as permitted. My carry-on is always as large as allowed, and I want to get it into an overhead storage compartment before they all fill.

Arrival at Destination Airport with Bikes

Picking up bikes

A cart holding bikes is usually too large for elevators and door-ways. Ask to use the freight elevator. I loop the bike lock cable through the bike box holes and then onto the cart so I can move more easily.

Picking up vehicle

After you pick up your baggage, go to the company counter where you have reserved your vehicle.

Camper van

If you've rented an camper van, ask at the car rental counter for detailed directions on where to pick up the camper van. If neither the hotel nor vehicle rental company can pick you up in a van, you'll need a special large taxi.

Car

If you've rented a car, take your bikes to an out-of-the-way place to reassemble them. Pick up your car. Attach the bike rack and bikes. Discard the cardboard boxes or arrange to store the hard sided boxes. (See "Storing Bike Boxes.")

Assembling the bikes

If you are picking up a car at the airport, you'll need to assemble your bike and bike rack in the airport parking lot. You'll be tired since you've just gotten off the plane, so clear directions and access to all necessary parts and tools are critical. Be sure you bring good tools for assembling and dismantling the bikes.

Before you leave on your trip, make a drawing of how the bikes should be put back in the boxes. Also make notes about how to reassemble the bikes.

Store this information carefully.

Tutoring from a knowledgeable biking person is essential if you are a beginner. It's a good idea to practice taking apart and reassembling your bike a few times before you leave home.

Storing bike boxes

Storing hard-sided bike boxes at the airport or train station is expensive. An alternative is to spend the first night in a hotel that provides van pick-up from the airport. After resting, assemble your bikes. Arrange to store the bike boxes at the hotel for the duration of the trip. Then either take the hotel van back to the airport to pick up your car, or take a taxi to the camper van pick-up site. Drive back to the hotel, put on your bike rack and bikes, and head out on your adventure!

Picking Up Your Vehicle

Whether you should pick up your vehicle right away or go to a hotel for the first night to rest before you start driving depends on your previous experience with driving in a foreign country. It's very important that you spend ample time learning about your vehicle before you leave the pickup site. When picking up an camper van, allow at least an hour and a half to learn and then practice all the things you need to know. It is also complicated to find your first camping place.

Ask questions

Ask questions at the vehicle pickup site. Having someone who explains how something works here is much easier than trying to figure it out later using a driver's manual that might be written in a foreign language.

Practice before leaving pickup site

Practice the following at the pickup site without someone helping you:

• Remove the key from the ignition.
• Operate the turn signals and windshield wipers.
• Turn the headlights, bright lights, and warning light on and off.
• Turn on the heater and air conditioner.

Checklist

• Check all tires for wear, including the spare.
• Examine the tools included with the vehicle.
• Ask how to remove the spare tire and change a tire.
• Make sure you have everything you need to change a tire.
• Ask how to fill the vehicle with gas and oil.
• Get a signed statement about existing dents, scratches and so on.

For camper van campers

Learn how by practicing:

• Taking the bed out
• Connecting to electricity
• Connecting to water
• Disposing of waste water
• Turning on the stove
• Turning the refrigerator to battery or electrical voltage
• Turning on the cabin lighting

These things might seem simple, but there are often little tricks that you learn through practice. Each person should try doing each of the procedures. If you have questions after doing this without help, get answers now. Don't be afraid to ask what seems like a silly question.

The Navigator's Job

Importance of
the navigator

The navigator's job is critical to the success of your trip. The driver can't navigate and drive too. So the navigator must be alert and mindful of the road at all times.

Driving out of
the vehicle
pickup site

Ask the personnel at the vehicle pickup site to direct you to your first destination. Always write down directions. Then reconfirm what you wrote down. Check directions against your map. Don't rush. Getting going in a strange country takes concentration. Ask which road signs to look for and the approximate mileage before you turn off.

Remember, you must be able to find the pickup site again when you return the vehicle. As you leave the vehicle pickup site, write down street names, names of buildings where you make turns, and highway exit signs. Put this where you can find it when you are returning. Also, turn around in your seat and look at what the road will look like when you are returning.

Always know
where you are
on the map

Always keep the map open and be able to point to where you are. Check street and highway signs to make sure you are going in the right direction.

Locate towns
on road signs on
your map

If you aren't absolutely sure where you are, have the driver pull to the side of the road in front of a highway sign. Find where you are on the map. Does the sign indicate that you are going in the right direction? Are the towns that are listed on the highway sign located in the direction you want to go? Find all the places that are listed on the sign on your map. The time it takes to check town signs with your map is little compared to the time you might otherwise have to spend correcting a mistake.

Continue
checking

Once you are positive you are going in the right direction, you still must be alert. Each time there is an exit sign for a street or town, find it on the map. This way you can catch a mistake early.

Read the map far ahead of where you actually are. Use the index to find towns and cities. Become familiar with the names of all the major towns in all directions. Highway signs often indicate towns located in several directions. Tell the driver where you don't want to go.

Give the driver warning about upcoming turns

When you are about ten minutes away from a turnoff, tell the driver the name of the turnoff and whether it will be a left or right turn. Remind the driver as you approach the turn. Anticipate what the road sign will say, and tell the driver so you both can look for signs. Occasionally the driver should also look at the map. The driver might notice something the navigator didn't.

Mistakes happen

Mistakes are going to be made. Be patient. Don't ruin the joie de vivre of the trip with anger. Learn from a mistake and try not to repeat it. Consider a mistake as part of your training in becoming a better navigator or driver.

International Road Signs

Priority Road Signs

Priority for oncoming traffic

Give way

Mandatory Signs

Compulsory roundabout

Prohibitory or Restrictive Signs

Closed to all vehicles in both directions

No entry

No entry for power-driven vehicles

No left turn

No right turn

Overtaking prohibited

Parking prohibited

Standing and parking prohibited

Limited duration parking zone

Useful Information Signs

Tourist information

Camping site

Camping and trailer site

Useful Information Signs (continued)

Hospital

Parking

One way

One way

Motorway

Direction to a camping site

Warning Signs

Dangerous bend: double bend

Dangerous bend: left bend

Uneven road: dip

Uneven road: hump, bridge, or ridge

Two-way traffic

Approach to intersection: roundabout

Approach to intersection: merging traffic

Approach to intersection: side road

Camping and Cooking

Finding the Camping Place

Allow enough time

If you don't read or speak the language of the country, allow an hour to find the camping place after you have gotten to the general area. Consider it part of the adventure, and allow for it in your day's time schedule.

Camping places are often in out-of-the-way places. Always find yours before you are tired, because the search takes a lot of energy and patience.

Getting directions

I look for residents who are walking or biking when I need directions. They know their neighborhood. These people are usually happy to help you. They want you to have a nice time in their country. Gas station attendants usually don't know more than the main highways.

Use fill-in forms for getting directions

Say "Excuse me" in the local language and show the person the filled-in "Asking for Directions" form (found at the end of each country'). Even if the person can't help you, the smiles and thank-yous you'll exchange are fun!

After getting directions, if you still aren't sure you are going the right way, ask someone else. Maybe the next person's directions will be better. And if you are getting closer, this next person's directions can be more detailed. Keep using the filled-in "Asking for Directions" form.

Registering at camping places

Plan to get to your camping place by 11 A.M. if it is in a popular place in season. Many camping place offices close for a lunch break and don't reopen until 2 P.M. Some close by 8 P.M. You'll need to give the check-in clerk a passport or camping carnet. Fees are based on the number of persons, whether you want electricity, and whether you have pets. Sometimes you might not be assigned a particular campsite, but instead will share a general area with other campers.

Tokens or change for showers

Showers often cost extra. Buy your tokens or get change for them when you register, as you might want a shower when the office is closed.

Communal dishwashing areas

Most camping places have communal areas to wash dishes. Sometimes there's even a communal hot plate for cooking.

"Second home" campers

Camping places often have a large number of permanent campers and people who use them as a second home. Sometimes overnight campers like yourself are few.

Grocery Shopping

Store hours
Small stores frequently close for lunch and are not usually open on Sunday. Plan ahead. Each morning, plan your whole day with regard to shopping, sightseeing, and camping place hours.

Markets
I like to shop each day for supplies. It's fun to shop in a foreign country and interesting to see what is in the markets. Open markets are particularly inspiring and reasonably priced, so I include those I've discovered. Most aren't open every day and usually are open only in the morning. What is grown locally will be the best bargain.

How much to buy
It's easy to buy too much. Keep storage and deterioration in mind. Buy only what you need for that day and perhaps the next. Keep your supplies to a bare minimum. The clutter of extra supplies is irritating when you have to continuously reposition them.

Shopping list
Keep a shopping list going.

How to shop
I start in the produce section for inspiration about what to cook that night. Then I add meat or fish and then pasta, rice, or polenta. Every time I put something in my basket I ask myself, "Do I really need this?" (If you are careful about what you buy, you can eat at a reasonable cost anywhere in the world.) I try to cook enough at dinner to have leftovers for lunch the next day.

Store procedures
In some stores a token is needed to release a cart. The procedure for buying produce varies. Sometimes there is an attendant who selects and puts the produce you want in a bag and marks its cost. You usually won't be able to touch and select as at home, particularly in the smaller markets.

Watch what others are doing and do the same.

Charge cards
You can use a charge card in most major chains. This is particularly convenient if you are moving from country to country because you don't have to change as much money into the local currency.

First shopping trip

Buy some of these items on your first shopping trip for basic supplies:

- Onions, garlic, potatoes, lemons
- Optional, depending on how long you want to store them: cabbage, carrots, green onions, eggplant, tomatoes, apples, fresh herbs
- Other: mayonnaise, mustard, rice, polenta, pasta, rice vinegar, olive oil, sugar, evaporated milk, coffee, tea, wine, canned tomatoes, parmesan cheese.
- Spices if you didn't bring them: salt, pepper, Italian mixed herbs, basil.
- Insulated food storage container/cooler

Setting Up A Tent Camp

The "bedroom/ living room"

Place the living room tarp in front of the assembled tent. Put rocks on corners to keep the tarp neat. This tarp helps keep the tent clean.

The "kitchen"

Lay down the kitchen tarp next to the living room tarp, and place rocks on the corners. Place a collapsible chair as a cushion in front of the stove area, leaving enough space to do your food prep. This cushioned seating makes a big difference in your enjoyment of cooking. Place the cooler perpendicular to your cushion so that you can reach into it easily. Hang up the plastic shower bag close to your work area. Put enough water in the basin to wash vegetables, and place within reach of the cushioned work seat. Place the cutting board in front of your cushioned work area. You are now ready to begin the food prep. Some music and a beverage can make this more fun.

Camp Cooking Hints

Initial steps in preparing to cook

Start by gathering all food ingredients, spices, utensils, pots, pans, and eating utensils that you will need for the meal so you don't have to hunt for these things after you start cooking. This also allows you to use the tops of storage areas for cooking prep.

Wash all the vegetables you bought that day in the basin. Wash greens first and place them right side up in a strainer to drain. Take out what you need from the cooler, then use the top of it to drain the rest of the vegetables. If you wash everything now, you won't have to do it again later. Start your vegetable and fruit prep. Place items that will be cooked together in one bowl.

Using less expensive meat

Braising is an excellent way to use a less expensive and less tender, yet flavorful, piece of meat. Trim it first. In order for it to be tender, you must remove all the membrane. (Membrane looks like skin.) You'll need a small, sharp knife for this job. Cut the meat into 1- to 1½-inch pieces. Make them similar in size so they cook evenly. Now your meat is "prepped" and ready to cook.

Braising meat   Begin by putting a small amount of oil in the sauté pan. Over high heat, let the oil get smoking hot. Now place the pieces of meat in the pan. If the pan is small, brown the meat a little at a time. Each piece must be flat in the pan with a bit of room around it so the meat will brown and the moisture is locked in. Turn the meat, browning it on all sides. Remove the pieces that are done and continue until everything is browned.

Braising locks in moisture and gives meat a nice color. If you put in too much meat at one time, the juices will run from the meat and it will "stew" without browning, giving it a gray color.

If you are including vegetables with the meat, brown them after the meat in several portions in the same pan so you don't lose the flavorful particles of meat left in the pan. You can add more vegetables at once to the pan than you did meat, but not more than one layer. Store the cooked meat and vegetables in a bowl with a cloth over it to keep them warm.

Finishing the cooking   When the meat and vegetables are braised, turn heat down to medium-low. Put all the meat and vegetables back in the pan to finish the cooking. Add salt and pepper and any other herbs or spices you want at this time. Then add enough wine, bouillon cubes, and water so that there is approximately one inch of cooking liquid in your pan. Cover with a tight-fitting lid and cook over a low heat. (Remember, bouillon cubes are salty, so don't use additional salt with them.) The time it takes to finish cooking depends on the type of meat and vegetables that you are using. Check by tasting. Tasting is vital to being a successful cook. Taste a lot and adjust accordingly. It's fun and helps to develop your palate.

Other tenderizing methods

- Marinating is beneficial for all types of meat and poultry, even fish. The amount of time necessary for marinating varies. Chicken and fish marinate in about half an hour. Lamb, beef, and pork take three to four hours and should be refrigerated during this time.

- Curing is great for pork. It's easy to do, but it must sit in the curing liquid with refrigeration for at least 24 hours.

MARINATION OIL FOR ALL MEATS AND BRUSHING OIL FOR FISH	½ cup olive oil 2 tablespoons vinegar 2 teaspoons lemon juice 2 cloves garlic 1 teaspoon salt

For meat: Rub marinating oil thoroughly into the meat. Let meat rest for a hour or more. Less tender cuts of meat profit from longer marination, up to 24 hours.

For fish: Rub fish lightly with the marinating oil just before cooking.

CURING LIQUID FOR PORK Place all ingredients in a sauce pan. Simmer for 5 minutes. Let cool. Place pork in a storage container. Pour curing liquid over pork just to cover. Keep pork refrigerated for 24 hours. Remove pork from curing liquid and cook as desired. Discard used curing liquid.

3 cups water
½ cup lemon juice
⅔ cup sugar
¼ teaspoon cinammon
1 tablespoon salt

Blanching vegetables
If you are using vegetables that need blanching—such as green beans, broccoli, potatoes or cauliflower—bring a pot of salted water to a boil. Place vegetables in the boiling water and cook until al dente.* Remove with a slotted spoon and place in a bowl. Save the hot water and use it to cook pasta or polenta or for soaking utensils and wetting a rag for wiping up work areas.

Sautéing vegetables and meat
Heat oil in sauté pan until smoking hot. Put the prepped meat into the hot pan (no more than one layer at a time). Let it brown on one side (15–20 seconds). Stir to brown another side. Continue until cooked. Remove to a bowl. Cook the onions and garlic next, the same way. Then add other prepped vegetables, herbs, and spices. Cook until tender and warm, then add cooked meat and stir until hot.

Cooking pasta
Place 4 times as much water in the pot as pasta. Add enough salt so the water tastes just salty. Cover pot and bring water to boil over high heat. Pour the pasta into the boiling, salted water, stir occasionally to keep pasta separated. When it is still slightly firm,

take it off the heat, put on a lid, and set aside. Cover with towel to keep warm. When you are ready to serve, drain the pasta and place on plates.

Cooking polenta Pour the hot water you have been using to blanch vegetables into a bowl. Use a measuring cup to measure back into the pot the amount of liquid you need. For every cup of polenta use four times that amount of liquid. Bring the water to a boil. Sprinkle the polenta into the measured boiling water, stirring constantly. Turn down the heat so that the cooking polenta makes just small bubbles. Stir frequently. When it is thick and smooth, remove from the heat and cover with a lid and then cover with a towel to keep it warm while you finish the rest of the meal.

Clean up as you go Wipe down and wash things as you go. When you are done eating, the only items you should have left to wash are the pots that still have food in them and your eating and drinking utensils. Keep a plastic bag close to the prep area for food scraps that are to be thrown away

Last steps before you eat Before you start to eat, put any food left in the pot into the sauté pan. Put water and a bit of soap in the pot and let it soak while you are eating. Soak any other unwashed cooking utensils in here, too.

The reward! Place pasta, rice, polenta, or potatoes on serving plates. Spoon the sautéed meat and vegetables over it. Enjoy!

Camping Recipes

Asterisked terms are defined at the end of the chapter.

BROCCOLI WITH RED PEPPERS AND OLIVES

1 bunch broccoli (1½ to 2 pounds)
1 red bell pepper
12 olives, pits removed

pot with lid
bowl

Cut broccoli stems from the bottom to the top to separate the florets. Cut off some of the stem, leaving about 2 inches attached to the floret. Try to keep the pieces the same size so that all require the same amount of cooking. Throw away the excess stem, or peel and use the top part. Cut the red pepper into pieces about half the size of the broccoli pieces. Cook broccoli in boiling water to al dente,* scoop out of water, and place in bowl. Pour dressing over warm broccoli and toss. Add red peppers and olives and toss again. Serve.

Dressing

4 tablespoons olive oil
1 tablespoon lemon juice (lemon keeps broccoli green)
1 clove garlic, chopped or pressed
1 tablespoon parsley, chopped
1 teaspoon marjoram, tarragon, or basil (optional)
¼ teaspoon red pepper flakes (optional)

POTATOES, BROCCOLI, AND ONIONS WITH FRESH HERB SAUCE

1 pound potatoes, scrubbed, peeled (optional), cut into 1½-inch pieces
1 pound broccoli, trimmed and cut as in recipe above
1 medium onion, sliced into 1½ inch pieces

small and large bowl
pot

Make fresh herb sauce and let sit at least one half hour. Place potatoes in bowl of water as you prepare them so they don't discolor. Cook all vegetables separately, scooping out of water so that water is saved each time. Remove to a bowl as they are cooked and pour sauce over them while they are warm. Cover so they stay warm. Toss together and serve.

Fresh Herb Sauce (Use another dressing if you don't have fresh herbs.)

¼ cup fresh tarragon
2 tablespoons green onion, chopped
1 clove garlic, chopped or pressed
½ tablespoon lemon zest,* chopped
1 cup olive oil
3 tablespoons vinegar
salt and pepper

CHICKEN WITH MUSHROOMS, CREAM, AND BRANDY

2 boneless, skinless chicken breasts, split in half
1 cup mushrooms, cut in half
¼ cup butter
¾ cup heavy cream
3 tablespoons brandy
salt and pepper

sauté pan
small bowl

Heat butter until it is foaming. Salt and pepper the chicken breasts. Brown chicken breasts gradually. Remove from pan. Add brandy, scraping up the particles of browned chicken. Cook the mushrooms. Add cream and simmer until it is reduced a little. Add the browned chicken and cook until it is done, 2 to 3 minutes.

CHICKEN WITH MUSHROOMS, WINE, AND FRESH HERBS

2 pounds chicken legs cut into legs and thighs
2 to 3 tablespoons olive oil
2 cloves garlic, sliced thin
1 sprig fresh rosemary
1 sprig fresh thyme
1 sprig fresh oregano
1 cup mushrooms, sliced in half
1 cup white wine
salt and pepper

sauté pan with lid
small bowl

Salt and pepper the chicken on all sides. Heat oil to almost smoking hot. Brown chicken a few pieces at a time. Remove from pan. Pour off excess fat and discard. Brown the mushrooms. Remove. Pour in the wine and stir to scrape up particles of browned chicken. Put all the chicken back in the pan. Place the sprigs of fresh herbs amongst the chicken. Cover and cook over medium heat for 8–10 minutes. Turn chicken pieces over and cook covered for another 8–10 minutes. Add mushrooms, cover, and cook until mushrooms and chicken are cooked. Remove herb stems.

RICE WITH APPLES, NUTS, AND RAISINS AND CITRUS VINAIGRETTE

2 cups rice, water
$\frac{1}{4}$ cup raisins soaked in $\frac{1}{2}$ cup hot water
$\frac{1}{4}$ cup chopped nuts
$\frac{1}{4}$ cup chopped apples (optional)
$\frac{1}{4}$ cup green onions
$\frac{1}{2}$ cup citrus vinaigrette
salt

pot and lid
large bowl

Put rice in pot. Cover with enough water so that when you touch the *top* of the rice, water comes up to the first knuckle of your index finger. Add 1 teaspoon salt. Cover and cook at medium-high heat until steam comes out from under lid. Turn off heat, but don't uncover pan. Let sit covered for 15 minutes on hot but turned off burner, Meanwhile chop nuts, green onions, and apple. When rice is cooked place in bowl. Add $\frac{1}{2}$ cup citrus vinaigrette while it is still warm. When rice has cooled, add fruit, onions, and nuts.

Citrus Vinaigrette	1 tablespoon grated orange peel 2 tablespoons orange juice 2 tablespoons lemon juice 1 teaspoon rice vinegar 1 tablespoon chopped cilantro, parsley, or fennel (optional) 1 tablespoon green onion 1½ cup olive oil

Combine ingredients in a jar and shake well. Makes 2 cups.

MUSHROOM,
ONION AND
POTATO SAUTÉ
OR SOUP

2 small or 1 large onion, cut into ½-inch pieces
1 pound potatoes, peeled or not, and cut into ¼-inch slices
¾ pound mushrooms cut into ¼-inch pieces or a small handful of
  dried porcini mushrooms soaked in warm water for ½ hour or
  longer
2 tablespoons fresh herbs (tarragon, thyme, or parsley are good)
  or 1 tablespoon dried herbs
olive oil

sauté pan
small bowl

Heat enough olive oil just to cover the bottom of pan. Sauté onions and mushrooms separately; place in a bowl and keep warm. Sauté potatoes. When tender, add mushrooms, onions, and herbs. Salt and pepper to taste.

For soup: Follow directions above, but when finished add 3 cups canned chicken stock or stock made from dissolved bouillon cubes, ¼ cup cream, ¼ cup white wine, and cook until the potatoes are soft.

Variation: Substitute kale for mushrooms. Cut the ruffled edge of the kale away from the stem and chop coarsely into about ¼-inch pieces. Add ½ teaspoon chili flakes. (You can substitute other vegetables such as broccoli, cauliflower, or zucchini.)

PASTA WITH CHERRY TOMATOES, GARLIC AND BASIL

1 pound pasta
4 cups cherry tomatoes, cut in half
1 cup green onions
½ cup basil, layer leaves on top of each other and slice crosswise (julienne*)
4 cloves garlic, chopped or pressed
olive oil
salt and pepper
parmesan cheese, grated

pot and lid
sauté pan

Place enough olive oil in sauté pan to just cover bottom. Heat until almost smoking hot. Add tomatoes, garlic, and green onions. Sauté about 1–2 minutes until just cooked. Remove the pan from the heat and add the sliced basil. (Cooking the basil with the rest of the ingredients will make it turn dark.) Bring 1½ quarts of water to boil, add 2 tablespoons salt to water, and cook pasta until al dente. Drain pasta, put on individual plates, and top with tomato sauce. Sprinkle with grated parmesan cheese.

Variation:

Add 2 tablespoons capers or olives. Substitute eggplant for the tomatoes or add eggplant.

Eggplant preparation

Cut eggplant crosswise into ¼-inch-thick round slices. Then cut the circles into ¼-inch pieces. Place eggplant in a colander. Salt fairly well and let sit for 1 hour. Squeeze bitter juice from the eggplant and then sauté like tomatoes in the hot olive oil.

PASTA WITH TOMATOES, GARLIC, AND BASIL

3 cups chopped fresh tomatoes or 1½ cups canned
½ cup olive oil
1 cup basil, thinly sliced, julienne
3 garlic cloves, thinly sliced
1 tablespoon finely chopped hot pepper or ½ teaspoon red pepper flakes (optional)
¾ pound pasta
1 tablespoon sugar
salt and pepper
parmesan cheese, freshly grated

pot and lid
sauté pan and lid

Heat olive oil in sauté pan. Add garlic and optional hot pepper. Cook garlic until golden brown. Remove from heat and add tomatoes, basil, salt, pepper, and sugar. Bring to boil 2½ quarts water for pasta. Set sauté pan on top of pot with boiling water for pasta. Heat sauce over water until just warm. Remove from heat and cover to keep warm. Cook pasta. Drain and toss with the sauce. Serve with freshly grated cheese.

SAUSAGES COOKED WITH BEER AND POTATOES

1 to 1½ pounds sausage
1 large onion, chopped
2 cloves garlic, thinly sliced
2 medium potatoes, sliced ¼-inch-thick, peeled or unpeeled
    (keep in water until ready to use so they don't discolor)
3 tablespoons olive oil
½ bottle of beer
1 tablespoon dried basil or tarragon

pot and lid
sauté pan and lid
bowl

Boil sausages in water until just firm, about 6–8 minutes. Remove sausages and place sliced potatoes in boiling water. Cook 1–2 minutes until just slightly soft. Remove from water. Discard water or save for another use. Slice sausages into 1-inch pieces. Heat olive oil in sauté pan until almost smoking hot, add onions, and turn down heat to medium. Add garlic, stir into onions, and cook until onions are translucent. Add sausage pieces to the top of the onions. Layer potatoes over the sausages. Pour beer over the top. Sprinkle dried or fresh herbs over the potatoes. Cover and cook over medium-low heat until potatoes are cooked, about 15 minutes.

SWEET CHICKEN WITH TOMATOES AND OLIVES

2 whole skinless and boneless chicken breasts, split and cut into
    2-inch pieces
1 large onion, chopped fine
2 garlic cloves, sliced thinly
3 tomatoes, chopped coarsely
1 tablespoon maple syrup or honey
1 tablespoon dried basil
1 teaspoon dried red pepper flakes (optional)
½ cup white wine

¼ cup olives
3 tablespoons olive oil

sauté pan
bowl

Heat oil to almost smoking hot. Brown chicken pieces gradually. Remove from pan. Lower heat to medium and add onions, garlic, and red pepper flakes. Cook until onions are translucent. Add browned chicken, tomatoes, basil, syrup or honey, and olives. Cook on medium heat covered. Stir occasionally.

TUSCAN BEEF STEW

2 pounds beef chuck or round steak, well trimmed and cut into
   1-inch pieces
1 large or 2 small onions cut in 1-inch pieces
1 pepper (red is preferable) cut in 1-inch pieces
2 cloves garlic, thinly sliced
1 carrot, peeled and cut in ¼-inch slices
1 cup white or red wine
¼ cup olive oil
1 teaspoon lemon or orange zest* (optional)
1 tablespoon dried basil
salt and pepper to taste

sauté pan

Heat the olive oil until it is almost smoking hot. Place meat gradually into the hot oil, allowing space between pieces so that it browns well. Turn until all the sides are browned. Remove the meat from the pan when browned on all sides and continue cooking until all the meat is finished. Turn down heat to medium. Add onions, stirring and scraping the bottom of the pan so that all the browned bits of meat are incorporated with the onion. Add the sliced garlic, peppers, carrots, basil, and zest. Stir to blend vegetables together. Cook on medium heat until onion is translucent. Add meat, wine, and salt and pepper. Cook covered until meat is tender, half an hour to an hour depending on the cut. Serve over rice, pasta, potatoes, or polenta.

TUSCAN MEAT SAUCE FOR SPAGHETTI

1 pound ground beef or pork
1 large onion, finely chopped
2 cloves garlic, thinly sliced
1 medium carrot, grated
1 fennel bulb, finely chopped
1 tablespoon fennel seed, toasted
⅓ cup olive oil
2 cups fresh tomatoes, chopped, or 1 cup canned
½ cup red or white wine
1 pound pasta
salt and pepper
¼ teaspoon hot pepper flakes or 1 tablespoon fresh hot pepper, chopped
parmesan cheese, freshly grated

sauté pan
pot and lid
bowl

Heat pan over high heat. Gradually add ground meat so it has a bit of room in the pan and browns, rather than stews and turns gray. Remove meat from pan and keep warm. Discard fat left in pan. Heat olive oil in pan to almost smoking hot. Add onion, and turn down heat to medium, stirring and scraping up brown pieces of meat. Add garlic, carrot, fennel, fennel seed, and wine. Cook over medium heat until vegetables are soft and have cooked together, about 20–30 minutes. Add cooked meat and tomatoes. Salt and pepper to taste. Let simmer 10–15 minutes.

Fill pot with water. Add 1 tablespoon salt. Cover pan and bring water to boil over high heat. Cook pasta. Drain, place on plates, ladle meat sauce on top, and serve with freshly grated parmesan cheese.

PROVENÇAL VEGETABLE STEW OR SALAD

2 medium carrots, peeled and cut diagonally, ¼-inch thick and 2 inches long
¾ pound asparagus or broccoli (optional), cut 2 inches long
¼ pound snow peas or sugar snaps (optional), ends trimmed
2 medium zucchini, washed and cut diagonally, ¼-inch thick and 2 inches long
1 pound green beans, cut 2 inches long
1 onion (if making stew), cut into size similar to rest of vegetables
4 garlic cloves, pressed or chopped (if making stew)
2 tablespoons olive oil (if making stew)
water

salt and pepper
1 cup Lemon Vinaigrette (if making as salad)

pot and lid
sauté pan (if making stew)
large bowl

Fill pot with water. Add 1 tablespoon salt. Cover pot and bring water to boil over high heat. Place one type of vegetable (except onion and garlic) in the boiling water at a time. When vegetables are cooked al dente,* remove by scooping from boiling water and place together in large bowl. Use the same boiling water to cook each type of vegetable. (The different vegetables take different amounts of time to cook, so it is necessary to cook them separately.)

For stew: As each vegetable is cooked, place in a bowl. Put foil over bowl so vegetables stay warm as you cook the rest. In large sauté pan, heat olive oil over medium-high heat. Add onions and garlic. Sauté until onions are translucent. Add cooked vegetables and stir together. Salt and pepper to taste.

For salad: As each vegetable is cooked, add a bit of Lemon Vinaigrette while the vegetable is still warm. Toss gently to cover vegetables. Salt and pepper when all vegetables are cooked and dressed.

LEMON VINAIGRETTE

1 teaspoon lemon peel
1 tablespoon parsley, chopped
1 tablespoon green onions
juice of 1 lemon
¾ cup olive oil
clove garlic, pressed
salt and pepper

Place in covered jar and shake. Makes one cup

MUSTARD VINAIGRETTE

1 cup olive oil
2 tablespoons vinegar
1 tablespoon Dijon-type mustard
1 or 2 cloves garlic, pressed
salt and pepper

Variations:	Use ½ walnut oil instead of all olive oil. Use different kinds of vinegars: raspberry for salad with fruit, balsamic with full-flavored greens or vegetables, or rice for lighter vegetables and greens.

HERB VINAIGRETTE

Add up to ¼ cup chopped herbs to Mustard Vinaigrette. Herbs can be mixed or all of one type. Chervil, basil, parsley, chives, dill, tarragon, and mint are all nice. Chopped green onions can also be added. (To decide if herbs go well together, smell the different herbs and decide if they are compatible.)

CHEESE VINAIGRETTE

Add ¼ cup loosely crumbled cheese to Mustard Vinaigrette. Gorgonzola, feta, blue, and parmesan all work well.

Cooking Definitions

Al dente: Cooked until softened but still has some firmness.

Braise: To brown food on all sides in a small amount of hot oil or fat. (Cook in small portions if necessary so that there is space between each piece and the food browns rather than stews. Remove browned pieces and add the rest gradually until all are browned. Return all food pieces to pan. Add liquid to almost cover food. Lower heat to simmer. Cover until cooked.)

Juilenne: Cut into lengthwise strips ⅛-inch wide.

Sauté: Brown and cook food in a small amount of hot oil or fat in an uncovered pan.

Toast: Cook in sauté pan over medium heat until fragrant. (Stir frequently.)

Zest: Colored (not white) part of citrus peel, usually chopped or sliced thinly.

Countries to Visit

Austria

This beautiful country combines stunningly scenic countryside with a sophisticated city life of music and culture.

Best time to go   Many camping places are open only May through September. They are most crowded in July and August.

Camping places   Camping places are plentiful. Those located close to major cities are often open all year, as are some close to ski areas. Many in the Alpine regions are open only May through September.

Driving   Roads are good. However, there are many mountainous routes and some long tunnels. Take extra care on these routes during rainstorms and unseasonable snow. The toll roads are expensive, but the scenery is spectacular.

Tourist offices   These offices are staffed by friendly and helpful people. Someone who speaks English will be available. Called Verkehrsverein or Verkehrsamt, tourist offices are located in the town center and at the main autobahn exits. They are a good source for maps, as well as information on camping places, museums, castles, concerts, plays, and hiking.

Shop hours	Generally shops open by 9 A.M. and close around 6 P.M. In small towns shops often close for a couple hours for lunch and on Saturdays are generally open just in the morning. Shop early, Saturdays will be crowded.
Eating out	Austrian food is hearty, and the pastries are exquisite. The special menu for the day is called Tagesteller or Tagesmenu and is always reasonably priced. Wine cellars, or Heurigen, usually have inexpensive meals.

SALZBURG Home to Mozart and setting for *The Sound of Music,* Salzburg is a masterpiece of architecture and gardens set on the River Salzach.

Interesting are:

- The old town walking tour. Get a map at the tourist office.
- Hohensalzburg Castle. Besides providing a wonderful view of the city from its tower, this castle has state rooms, torture chambers, and several museums. The guided tour is quite good.
- Mirabell Gardens, Palace, and Orangery. They are charming in their quiet elegance.
- Live musical performances. In such a musical city, it's worth the effort to attend a performance.
- Beer halls. My favorite is Augustiner Braustubl, at 4-6 Augustinergasse. To reach it, you climb a steep cobblestone street, then enter a nondescript building and descend a staircase to a hallway of little kiosks selling wonderful beer-cellar food. In summer the beer is poured into big stone mugs in a garden. In winter it is served in one of several huge cellars.
- Helbrunn Palace, Gardens, Zoo, and Folklore Museum. This whimsical side trip just south of the city is particularly fun for families.

Camping places
- In city center: Stadt Camping, Bayerhammerstrasse 14A
- Close to the city center, with a lovely view of the city: Camping Stadtblick, Rauchenbichlerstr. 21
- In Langmoosweg, in a garden setting: Camping Nord-Sam, Samstr. 22-A
- North of A1 Nord exit: Kasern Camping Kasern, 1
- Verkehrsverein, Mozartplatz 5

Food markets
- At Mirabellplatz, Thursday
- In Universitatsplatz, weekdays and Saturday morning

Salzkammerg Ut Region

Located just east of Salzburg, this mountainous area is dotted with lakes. Most camping places have "second home" camping. Hiking is very popular, and there are many well-marked trails. Cable cars can take you to summits, and you can then hike down. The scenery is spectacular, and biking is lovely along the lakes. Some of the lakes have rental wind-surfing and sailing equipment.

Camping places
• Along the Wolfgangsee in Abersee: Camping Wolfgangblick, Abersee 24, and Camping Lindenstreand, Gschwand 36

Food market
On Friday afternoons, just north of Gmunden, between Puhrzaunstr. and Stelzerweg, off of Ohlsdorferstrasse

HALLSTATT
This tiny, picture-perfect village is situated alongside a lake within a deep gorge. Salt mines and giant ice caves are close by.

Camping place
• Campingplatz Klausner-Holl, Lahnstrasse 6

SALZBURGER SPORTWELT AMADE
This lovely resort area is well known for its skiing and hiking. A short walk through the Liechtensteinklamm, a magnificent narrow gorge just south of St. Johann, passes a spectacular waterfall.

Camping place
• In St. Johann, signs posted from the train station: Camping Weiesof

VIENNA
Those who love the arts love Vienna. It was the home of Strauss, Mozart, Beethoven, Brahms, Haydn, and Schubert. There are wonderful palaces, museums, concert halls, and theaters. Walking and biking are especially rewarding here.

Be sure to see:
• St. Stephens cathedral. It is architecturally impressive, with a steeple and expressive statues.
• The Imperial Palace. This has an incredible collection of both treasures and relics.
• Schonbrunn Palace. A good place for learning about court life during the Hapsburg Empire.
• A musical performance. So that you can better appreciate the great composers who were inspired here.

- The Kunsthistorisches Museum. World famous, this houses one of the world's best collections of sixteenth and seventeenth century paintings, ornaments, and glassware. To be in Vienna and not see it would be like being in Paris and missing the Louvre.
- The Spanish Riding School. A must see for horse-lovers and families

In between all this sightseeing you can rest your mind and feet while sipping fragrant Viennese coffee and nibbling on the area's fabulous desserts.

Camping places
- In Hutteldorf: Wien West I and II, Huttenbergstrasse 80; bus available to city center
- In Kaisermuhlen, close to Prater Amusement area: Camping Neue Donau; bus available to city center

Tourist offices
- In city center at Karntner Strasse 38
- At autobahn A1 exit Wein-Auhof
- At autobahn A2 exit Zentrum
- At autobhan A4 exit Simmerig-Haide

Food market   Naschmarkt, 6 Linke Wienzeile, daily

INNSBRUCK   The capital of the Tirol is set between the Alps and Tuxor Mountains, making it an ideal hiking and skiing area. Stubal Glacier has skiing all year. The tourist office provides free mountain guidebooks as well as extensive information on cultural activities and exhibits.

Camping places
- In the city, signs posted from the train station, close to the hostel: Campingplatz Reichenau on Reichenauerstrasse and Camping See wirt on Amras Geyrstrasse
- West of town center in Kranebitte: Camping Innsbruck Kranebitten, Kranebitten Alle

Tourist offices
- Tirol Information Office at Wilhelm Greil Strasse 17
- Main office, Burggraden 3

Food market
Large indoor market; by the river in Markthalle, directly behind the Altstadt Herzog Siegmund Ufer

Lechtaler Alps

Located in the northwestern Tirol on the German border, these breathtakingly beautiful Alpine mountains have some of the best skiing in the world. There are plenty of chair lifts, and guided hiking trips are available.

Camping places
- In Reutte, signs posted from the train station: Camping Sintwag
- On shores of Plansee, in Seespitze: Camping Seespitze, Blandseestrasse 72
- On the shores of Plansee, at Forelle: Camping Sennalpe
- In Landeck, on the Sanna River: Camp Riffler

KITZBUHEL   This fashionable and prosperous little town is well known for its ski slopes and gorgeous countryside. Alpenblumengarten, a lovely area where many species of alpine flowers can be enjoyed, can be reached via the Kitzbuheler Hornbahn lift.

Camping place   • In Schwarzsee, close to the lake: Camping Schwarzsee

Food market   In front of the tourist office, Wednesdays and Saturday mornings

ZELL AM ZELLER   Set along the Ziller River, this popular hiking area has cable cars and chair lifts to transport you up to grassy meadows for hiking. The friendly, small-town atmosphere is charming. Check with the tourist office for information about folk-singing festivals, band concerts, and guided hiking.

Special are:

• Krimmler Waterfall. Located in the Hohe Tauern National Park, this is the highest waterfall in Europe.

• Grossglockner Strasse. The famous mountain road provides a spectacular drive through Alpine valleys where you will see meadows blanketed with wildflowers, dramatic waterfalls, and a glacier. Note that there are many hairpin turns on this narrow road. Consider a bus tour. If you do drive, be prepared for a heavy toll charge.

Camping places   • In Zell Am Zeller: Campingplatz Hofer, Gerlosstr. 33

• In Zell am See/Prielau, on the lake: Camping Seecamp, Thumersbacherstr. 34

• In Zell am See: Camping Sudufer, Seeuferstr; not as nice as the above but less expensive

LEINZ   (*not to be confused with Linz*)
Known for its rock band concerts, this relaxed town is also popular with hikers. The tourist office has information about current musical performances and other events.

Camping place   • South of town across the Drau River, close to the soccer and track fields: Camping Falken, Eichholtz 7

German

Guten tag

Hello

Bitte, wo ist _____?

Please, where is _____?

Konnen sie es bitte aufschreiben.

Could you please write it down.

Gehen Sie geradeaus _____ (meters/kilometers) zu _____ (sehen Liste Ich Verstehe).

Go straight ahead _____ (meters/kilometers) to _____ (see List I Understand).

Biegen Sie _____ (rechts/links) gehen _____ (meters/kilometers) zu _____ (sehen Liste Ich Verstehe).

Turn _____ (right/left) go _____ (meters/kilometers) to _____ (see List I Understand).

Nachste biegen _____ (rechts/links) gehen _____ (meters/kilometers) zu _____ (sehen Liste Ich Verstehe).

Next turn _____ (right/left) go _____ (meters/kilometers) to _____ (see List I Understand).

Wie weit ist? _____ (minutes/stundes)

How long will it take? _____ (minutes/hours)

Danke

Thank you

List I Understand	**Liste Ich Verstehe**
corner	ecke
stop sign	stop zeichen
traffic light	stop signal
exit	ausgang
road/street	strade
highway	autostrada
large	gross
small	klein
far	weit
near	nahe
bridge	brucke
river	flub
woods	wald
lake	see
sea	mer
harbor	hafen
village	ort
town/city	stadt
house	haus
train station	bahnhof
bus stop	bushaltestelle
red	rot
green	grun
blue	blau
yellow	geld
white	weiss
black	schwarz
market place	marketplatz
supermarket	supermarket
gas station	benzin
square	platz
main square	haupplatz
castle	schloss
cathedral	Dom
church	kirche
camping place	campingplatz
old town	alstadt
museum	museum

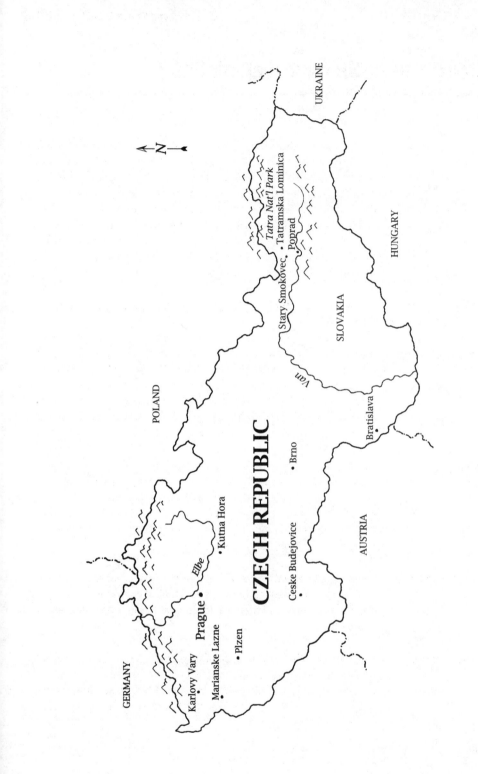

Czech and Slovak Republics

Located in the center of Europe, this is a wonderful area to visit if you love fine architecture, music, and the outdoors. Forty well-preserved towns feature exceptional architecture and winding cobblestone streets. You can visit more than four thousand castles, some fully restored and with adjoining museums.

Here you'll find international film festivals, exceptional operas, and world-class symphonies at reasonable prices. The area's outstanding natural beauty includes lakes, rivers, caves, and the magnificent Tatra mountains—waiting to be explored and enjoyed.

Best time to go
The weather is best from April through November. It is warmer on the coast.

Camping places
Plentiful camping places are found close to all tourist areas and throughout the country at lakes, rivers, and mountain areas. They are generally open May through September. There are not as many amenities in the camping places here as you find in Western Europe, but they are usually located in lovely spots, are not overly crowded, and are reasonably priced.

Driving
Not heavily trafficked, this area is easy to drive in. Roads and camping places are well marked. The landscape is lovely, and the local people will go out of their way to help you find your destination. Parking restrictions, speed limits, and general driving rules are similar to those in the United States. If you are ticketed and fined, be sure to ask for a receipt.

Tourist offices
Cedok travel agents operate as tourist offices, but they are oriented to tourists staying in hotels and taking guided tours. Bring a good guide book and then ask for help at the receptionist desk of a large hotel.

Food markets
Food, wine, and beer are available at reasonable prices. Vegetables are grown locally, but choices aren't as varied as in Western Europe. Meat quality is good. You must shop first thing in the morning to get a good selection. If you can, stock up in the larger cities.

To find supermarkets, look for housing complexes. Often there are a few farmers selling their produce outside the supermarket. On Saturday mornings you might see a line. This is not because there is a food shortage; it's because the store can handle only so many people at a time, and people must wait their turns.

Shop hours   They are generally open from 9:00 A.M. to 6:00 P.M. Smaller stores may close for lunch. Shop in the mornings to get the best selection.

Bohemia

Bohemia is known for its architecture and history. Spa resorts and beer-making centers are plentiful.

Outstanding places to visit include:

- The State Jewish Museum in Prague. This is the largest and most authentic Jewish museum in Europe.
- The Technological Museum in Brno. The museum houses the wonderful 1890 panorama.
- The Slovak National Uprising Museum in Banska Bystrica. The museum documents a historic period in the country.
- The Tatra National Park Museum in Tatranka Lomnica. It tells about what you'll experience on your walks and hikes.
- The Karlstejn and Cesky Krumlov castles. These are architectural wonders.

Note that museums and castles are usually closed on Mondays.

PRAGUE   Prague is one of the most beautiful and well-preserved medieval cities in Europe.

Be sure to:

- walk across the Charles Bridge into Stare Mesto (old town). You will pass beautiful old churches and homes of the nobility as you stroll into the heart of the old city square.
- walk up to the Prague Castle, which looms over city offering fabulous views. See the treasury in the Loreta Convent, which is close by.

- walk or bike along the Vltave (Moldau) River, which meanders through Prague. See the Mala Strana, which has lovely baroque homes of old nobility.
- experience the beer halls, which are lively and plentiful. The beer garden U Fleku, at Kremencova 11, is touristy but fun. Their dark beer is excellent. A cabaret hall is next door.

Konopiste Castle and gardens with its outstanding collection of hunting trophies and weapons is close to Prague, in Benesov.

There's camping in the grounds adjacent to the park.

Tourist office

Prague Information Center (PIS), Na Prikope 20. Pick up a tourist map of the city that has the metro stops of the main tourist sights, as well as a guide to the exceptional historic walks. The public transit system is good, and you might want to use it. Be sure to ask about musical performances and other cultural activities.

Camping places

All are close to public transport to city center.

- West of the city, off Plzenska, at TJ Vysoke Skoly: Sportcamp
- North of Prague in Troja, several
- West of city center, near Sarka valley: Aritma Dzban, Nad lavkou 3, Vokovice; tents only
- South of city, on the Vltara: U ledaren 55, Branik

KUTNA HORA

The Hradek Mining Museum with its huge medieval mining shafts is fun to visit. Visitors wear white coats and helmets with miners' lamps for the 500-meter trip into the shafts.

KARLOVY VARY

Beethoven, Brahms, Bismark, Chopin, Goethe, Liszt, Tolstoy, and many other famous people have partaken of the healing waters in this famous spa town. You can walk the same quiet, elegant streets they did. You'll also see lovely parks and beautiful homes through-out the wooded hills. Bring a cup so you can sample the healing water from the colonnade on the main walking street. It gushes water at 2,000 liters a minute. An afternoon swim at the open-air mineral pool, or bazen, on the hill above the Thermal Sanatorium is especially nice.

Camping place

- South of the spa center, along Highway 20 in the direction of Plzen, close to the Gejzirpark Hotel and Motel Brezova (There are hot showers and tennis courts at the Gejzirpark Hotel that are open to the public.)

MARIANSKE LAZNE

This famous spa area is much smaller and less sophisticated than Karlovy Vary. Its higher elevation gives it an alpine feeling and makes it a nice area for hiking as well.

Camping place

• South of town at Velka Hledsebe: Autocamp Luxor

PLZEN

A must-see for beer lovers, this large industrial town has brewed Pilsner for 700 years. The Museum of Beer Brewing is located in an authentic Malt House in the old town, close to the Mze River. Take a walk around the old town. For an interesting diversion, visit the Underground Corridors, which once provided underground refuge; they are close to the museum. From there walk over to the famous Urqueil Brewery. There are plenty of good places to enjoy beer while you're here.

Camping place

• North of the city in Bila Hora, on Highway 27: Camping Bila Hora

CESKE BUDEJOVICE

Located halfway between Plzen and Vienna, this lovely medieval town is the original home of Budweiser beer.

Notable are:

• The palace at Hluboka nad Vltavou. Exceptionally well restored, this neo-Gothic palace has 144 rooms—some with the original furnishings. A fine art museum is now inside the palace's former riding school, and adjoining the palace is a beautiful park.

• Cesky Krumlov. Built during the Renaissance on the Vltava River, this is considered to be one of the most lovely towns in Europe. Its huge chateau is second only to the Prague Castle, and it has lovely gardens and courtyards as well.

Camping places

• Southwest of Ceske Budejovice, on the way to the airport: Dlouhe Louce Autocamp, Stromovka 8 and Stromovka Auto-camp, on Litvinoska

Moravia

This area is filled with wineries, theaters, and art galleries.

BRNO

Located halfway between Budapest and Prague, Brno has an abundance of cultural performances, art galleries, excellent museums, and castles.

Important here are:

- The Technological Museum (houses the 1890 panorama).
- Slavkov u Brna (Austerlitz) just east of Brno. This is where Napoleon Bonaparte defeated the armies of Austria and Russia. In the chateau an exhibit depicts Napoleon's life.
- Ballet and opera performances. Tickets can be bought in a small ticket office behind the Mahenovo Theatre.

Camping places

- Northwest of Brno, by Brno Dam: Veverska Bityska, scenic location
- South of Brno just beyond Modrice, on Highway 2 in the direction of Breclav: Autocamp Bobravia

Food market

On the street in front of the monastery at Zelny trh.

Slovakia

In Slovakia the combination of the magnificent Tatra mountains and peasant traditions make a visitor's experience here seem untouristy. Here you can enjoy the Vratna Valley, where the Tatra National Park is located.

Chair lifts are located at:

- Chata Vratna, a good place to start hiking
- Stary Smokovec, which goes up to Hrebienok for a spectacular view
- Tatranska Lominica, which goes up to Skalnate Pleso (This is popular; arrive early at Grandhotel Praha to purchase tickets.)
- Museum of the Tatra National Park, in Tatranska Lomnica

Camping places
- None in the National Park
- In the center of Vratna Valley, near Restauracia Stary Dvor
- Close to Stary Smokovec, on the road to Poprad-Tatry: Tatra Camping
- Below Strbske Pleso at Tatranska Strba
- Close to Tatranska Lomnica, near the railway station: Eurocamp FICC, very large; two smaller ones are Tatranec Campground and Sportcamp

Chalets

Adventurous and energetic hikers might want to get reservations at an alpine chalet, or chata. The sleeping arrangements are usually dormitory style, and breakfast is included in the very reasonable price. Bring snacks.

Chalet reservations can be hard to get as they are booked well in advance. You can try at the Cedok office in Stary Smokovec at Bilikova, Sliezky dom, and Moravku.

River rafting

Scenic rafting is available at the Dunajec River Gorge between the Slovak village of Cerveny Klastor and the Polish town of Szczawnica. The limestone cliffs make the scenery impressive. Trips can be arranged through a Cedok or at the raft office on the river at Cerveny Klastor. You can return via a walking path along the river, or you can walk to the nearby town of Stra Lubovna and take a regular scheduled bus back to Cervany Castor. There is camping on the river in Cerveny Klastor just down from the monastery.

BRATISLAVA

The Danube River flows through the capital of Slovakia, a fine historic town. Besides excellent opera productions, art galleries, and castles, it has a larger cultural center—the Dom Odborov. You can purchase opera tickets at the ticket office behind the National Theatre.

Camping places

• Northeast of the city, on the way to the airport, at Zlate piesky; one camping place is right at the lake, the other is close to the lake.

Tourist office

Off Hviezdoslavovo namestie, on the corner of Laurinska and Rybarska

Czech/Slovak

Ahoj

Hello

Prosim, kde _____?

Please, where _____?

Prosim muzete to napsat.

Please write it down.

Rovene _____ (meters/kilometers) do _____ (ukazte mi Liste Rozumim).

Straight ahead, _____ (meters/kilometers) to the _____ (show me on List I Understand).

Napravo/Nalevo _____ (meters/kilometers) do _____ (ukazate mi Liste Rozumim).

Go right/left _____ (meters/kilometers) to _____ (show me on Liste I Understand).

Napravo/nalevo _____ (meters/kilometers) do _____ (ukazate mi Liste Rozumim).

Go right/left _____ (meters/kilometers) to _____ (show me on List I Understand).

Jak dlouho trva cesta? _____ (minuty, hodin)

How long will it take? _____ (minutes/hours)

Dekuji

Thank you

List I Understand	Liste Rozumim
corner	rohu
stop sign	stop
traffic light	semaforu
exit	vychod
street/road	ulice
highway	dalnice
large	velike
small	male
far	daleko
near	blizko
bridge	most
river	reka
lake	jezero
town/city	mesto
train station	nadrazi/stanica
bus stop	autobusova zastavka
red	cerveny
green	zeleny
blue	modry
yellow	zluty
white	bily
black	cerny
market place	trh
supermarket	samoobsluha
gas station	benzinova pumpa
main square	hlavni namesti
castle	hrad
cathedral	katedrala/Dom
church	kostel
camping place	autokemp
old town	stare mesto
museum	museum
beach	plaz
building	budova
palace	palac
stadium	stadion

Denmark

This is the liveliest of the Scandinavian countries. Its music festivals, excellent museums, picturesque villages, magnificent castles, white sand beaches, and Viking artifacts make it a delightful country to visit. There are extensive bicycling routes over relatively flat countryside. English is commonly spoken.

Best time to go   Denmark has a temperate climate, so the weather is good from early summer to early fall. The fields are colorful in May and June. There are scores of music festivals and much street entertainment in July and August. The Danes vacation in July, so camping places will be more crowded.

Camping places   Camping is very popular with the Danes. Almost every town has at least one camping place. Bring an international camping carnet card (See Appendix: "Documents"), or buy a Danish camping card at the first camping place. Some farmers allow tent camping on their property. Pick up "*Overnataning i det fri,*" a list of such farms, at the tourist office. Many camping places also have cabins—handy for tent campers when it rains. Besides being clean and well run, the camping places often have communal kitchens, TV rooms, and small grocery shops. Tourist offices give out a free brochure listing the Danish camping places and basic camping place rules.

Driving   The excellent roads are well marked and not heavily trafficked, so driving is not difficult. The most reasonable gas is along motorways in the self-service stations. There is an extensive ferry system. Pick up a timetable at the tourist office. A ferry ticket for a car costs about three times as much as a ticket for a person.

Parking   Parking discs are used in small towns. (See Appendix: "Parking.") In large cities daytime parking is paid by buying a ticket at a street ticket machine. Look for a ticket machine in the area. Insert coins to advance to the time you will leave. Push the button to receive your ticket. Place it face up on your windshield. Parking is usually free after 6 P.M. on weekdays, after 2 P.M. on Saturdays, and all day on Sundays. Blue and green zones are less expensive than red zones.

Bicycling	Cities and towns have cycling lanes, and there are extensive routes throughout the country. It's an excellent way to get around. Bike rental is reasonable and readily available. Train stations and bike rental companies allow bikes to be rented in one town and dropped off at another. Pick up "*Cykelferiekort*," a map of cycling routes throughout the country, at the tourist office.
Open markets	Saturday and sometimes Wednesday markets are held in almost every town. Seek these out for more reasonably priced groceries. The tourist office will help with the exact location.
Tourist office	Generally located at the town hall (radhus) or town square (torvet). English is commonly spoken. The word *Slot* means castle.
Eating out	Danish restaurants are expensive; the best buy is the *dagens ret*, or daily special. The elaborate open faced sandwiches (*smorrebrod*) and pastries (*wienerbrod*) are hard to resist. Ethnic restaurants are reasonably priced and there are plenty of pizza places and snack stands. A 15 percent service charge is added to the bill, so you won't need to leave an extra tip.

Zealand

COPENHAGEN   The liveliest city in Scandinavia, this city has plenty of attractions. A sightseeing bus allows you to get on and off as you like at the main sights.

The most popular are:

- Tivoli. This hundred-year-old, classy amusement park has a fairy-tale atmosphere at night. Lovely gardens, entertainment, outdoor dining and rides make it special.
- Stroget. The world's largest pedestrian mall; this is a lively place to stroll.
- Ny Carlsberg Museum. It houses an excellent collection of Greek, Egyptian, and Etruscan sculpture, as well as paintings by Gauguin, Monet, and Van Gogh.
- Nationalmuseet. See the interesting collection of Viking, Bronze, and Stone Age artifacts.
- Rosenborg Slot. This castle houses the crown jewels and other Renaissance treasures. There is an excellent botanical garden and glass house with tropical plants on the west side.

- Small museums. Get "Copenhagen This Week" for detailed descriptions of a wide variety of fascinating collections.
- Carlsberg Brewery Tour.
- Canal Trip. Netto Badene Canal trips, opposite the stock exchange at Holmens Kirke, are the most reasonable.
- Open-air concerts. Get "Copenhagen This Week" from the tourist office. The ten-day Copenhagen Jazz Festival in July features well-known performers.

Close by attractions

- Louisiana Museum of Modern Art. This world-class museum is architecturally striking in its harmony with nature. It is just north of Copenhagen in Humlebaek.
- Dragor. This Dutch fishing town has thatched houses, winding cobblestone streets, fish markets, smokehouses, and a maritime museum. It is on the island of Amager, just south of the airport.
- Frilandsmuseet. Country houses, workshops, and barns are open to the public. It is in Lyngby, Kongevejen 100.

Tourist office

- Use It, in the Huset at Radhusstraede 13: best budget traveler information center (Get "Playtime," a free general guide.)
- North of the train station, at Berstoffsgade 1: a regular tourist office

Camping places

- Closest to the city, near the Bellahoj hostel: Bellahoj Camping, on Hvidkildevej; crowded
- Southwest of the city in Brondbyoster: Absalon Camping, Korsdalsvej 132
- In Naerum: Naerum Camping, on Ravnebakken; further away but pleasant

Food market

West of Norre Port train station on Israels Plat

Public transportation

Enter buses at the rear door. Buy a ticket from the machine. It will be good for an unlimited number of rides during the time period stamped on the ticket. The main terminals are close to the train and ferry stations.

Shop hours

Shops are generally open 9 A.M. to 5 P.M. weekdays, close early on Saturdays, and are closed on Sundays. Museums are closed on Mondays.

HILLEROD   North of Copenhagen, it is the site of the magnificent Frederiksborg Slot. The castle has elaborate gilded ceilings; a mammoth collection of paintings, tapestries, and furniture; an impressive coronation chapel, and a beautiful garden. A brochure-guide is helpful. Take the scenic road 152 from Copenhagen.

Camping place   • At Blytaekkervej

HELSINGOR   North of Copenhagen, just across from Sweden, its greatest attraction is Kronborg Slot. On the edge of the sea, the castle has an ornate chapel and royal chambers plus a gloomy dungeon lit with oil lamps.

Tourist office   Across Strangade from the train station, Havenpladsen 3

Camping place   • On the beach: Helsingor Camping, Sundtoldvej 9

ROSKILDE   West of Copenhagen, this fine small town has an outstanding Viking museum, Vikingeskibshallen, where five intricately restored Viking ships are displayed. Just southwest of the town, in Lejre, is the Historical Archaeological Experimental Center, where Danish families volunteer to dress in costume and live a daily life as people in the Iron Age. Visitors can try paddling in a dugout canoe, cooking flat bread, and grinding corn.

Camping place	• In Strandengen, on the banks of the Roskilde fiord.
Other popular places on Zealand (all have camping places)	• Mons Klint. It has dramatic white cliffs, neolithic burial sites with grave passages, and whitewashed churches with frescoes. • Hornbaek. Enjoy beaches and dunes. • Gilleleje: See the fish markets and smoke houses. • Naestved. There is river canoeing on River Susa. • Marielyst. This is a popular beach resort area.

Funen

It is called the garden island because of its many fruit orchards and vegetable farmlands, the rural landscape is dotted with old farmhouses.

ODENSE	This university city has interesting sights, pedestrian streets, and cycling lanes. Popular sightseeing: • Hans Christian Andersen Museum. See the memorabilia and books. • Den Fynske Landsby. This small country village, open to the public, has animals, orchards, furnished buildings, and flower gardens. • Jernbanemuseet. This is a railway museum. • Egeskov Slot. This Renaissance castle has a moat, drawbridge, peacocks, topiary, grass maze, and antique car museum. It is on route 8, close by in Kvaendrup.
Tourist office	At the Radhus, close to the train station
Camping place	• South of the city: Odense Camping, Odensevej 102

Jutland

On this island of windswept beaches, farmlands, and untouristed towns, popular sports are fishing, bicycling, and wind surfing.

ARHUS

A university town with some of the liveliest music and entertainment in Denmark, it has architecturally interesting buildings and a historic harbor.

Highlights are:

- Den Gamle By. This is a very large, reconstructed, old-fashioned Danish market town.
- Mosegard Prehistoric Museum. It has exhibits of Danish civilization from the Stone Age to the Viking Age. Highlights are the well-preserved 80 B.C. skeleton and the walk or tram ride through three kilometers of reconstructed prehistoric dwellings, monuments, and burial places.
- Musical festival in the first week of September.

Tourist office

In the Radhus, on Park Alle. Get tickets here for Ceres Brewery tours and the guide "What's On in Arhus." The cost of the guided tour covers a $2\frac{1}{2}$ -hour bus tour, entrance into Den Gamle By, and a 24-hour bus pass.

Camping places

- South of the city, by the bay, in Marselisborg woods: Blommehaven
- North of the city: Arhus Nord

RIBE

This is the oldest town in Scandinavia and is part of the National Trust. The picturesque tiny town is a living history museum. On the night watchman's tour, visitors accompany a costumed watchman who sings songs and tells stories of the old days.

Tourist office

At the back of the cathedral. Get the free "Denmark's Oldest Town" brochure for a self-guided tour.

Camping place

- At Farupvej

ROMO   Seals and wading birds are commonly spotted on this wind-swept coast close to Ribe. The historic town of Tonder has cobbled streets and gabled buildings. It hosts a jazz and blues festival at the end of August. Windsurfing is popular.

Camping place   • North of town, at Havnebyvey

Danish

Hallo

Hello

Ma jeg bede, behage hvor _____?

Please, where is _____?

Ma jeg bede, skrive.

Please, could you write it down.

Ga ligefrem _____ (meters/kilometers) til _____ (se List Jeg Forstar).

Go straight ahead _____ (meters/kilometers) to _____ (see List I Understand).

Farste dreje _____ (hojre/venstre) ga _____ (meters/kilometers) til _____ (se List Jeg Forstar).

First turn _____ (right/left) go _____ (meters/kilometers) to _____ (see List I Understand).

Naest dreje _____ (hojre/venstre) ga _____ (meters/kilometers) til _____ (se List Jeg Forstar).

Next go _____ (right/left) _____ (meters/kilometers) to _____ (see List I Understand).

Hvor _____ klokkeslet er der til?_____ (minuts/hvornars)

How long will it take? _____ (minutes, hours)

Tak

Thank you

List I Understand	Liste Jeg Forstar
corner	hjorne
intersection	gennemskaering
stop sign	stoppe maerke
traffic light	trafik
exit	sortie
road	vej
street	gade
highway	motorvej
large	stor
small	lille
far	fjern
near	naer
bridge	bro
river	flod
woods	skov
lake	lakfarve
harbor	havn
village	landsby
town	kobstad
city	stad
house	hus
train station	uddannue/opdrage
bus stop	omnibus stoppe
red	rod
green	gron
blue	bla
yellow	gul
white	hvid
black	sort
market place	markedsplads
gas station	benzin station
castle	borg
cathedral	domkirke
church	kirke
camping place	lejr
old town	gammel stad

France

A country of exceptional diversity and beauty, France is also historically important. Besides the famous museums and sights, there are many fascinating lesser-known ones.

Best time to go
As with most of central Europe, April through June and then September through October are the prime times to visit. There are fewer tourists then, and the weather is pleasant. Avoid going to popular beach areas in July and August and on any sunny weekend. Paris's weather is unpredictable; even in the summer it can be rainy one day and sunny the next.

Camping places
Because the French love to camp, there are camping places almost anywhere you might want to go. Avoid southern France in the months of July and August, when the locals take their vacations. Tourist offices in smaller towns sometimes have lists of *"camping a la ferme,"* or camping on the farm. Find your camping place before you go into a town or city, because the signs are posted along the roads coming into town.

Driving
French roads are wonderful, and there is an abundance of excellent secondary roads. The countryside is spectacular; so spend time in small towns and villages. Regular gas is called *essence* or super. Unleaded is *sans plomb* and diesel is *gasoil* or *gazole*. Gas purchased along the roads leading from small towns is least expensive.

Food markets
Prepared and packaged food is enticing but expensive. Meat is expensive, as are special cheeses. The recipes in this book use inexpensive cuts of meat. To save money, shop at the covered markets (Les Halles) and street markets.

Tourist offices
The tourist office is sometimes called *l'iniative*. The staff will speak some English and help with questions about unusual tours, walks, hikes, museums, bike or boat rentals, and open markets. *Vielle ville* means "old town."

Shop hours

Typically stores open between 9 A.M. and 10 A.M. and close between 6 P.M. and 7 P.M. In small towns, they close for lunch and open only in the morning on Saturdays. They are closed on Sundays. Museums are usually closed on Mondays.

Eating out

Use your guidebook to help you find a special place. Make reservations if possible. The gratuity will be included in the bill, but it is nice to leave a little extra if the service has been good.

Language

The French consider it polite for foreigners to use *merci* (thank you), *bonjour* (hello), *au revoir* (good-bye), and *pardon madame,* (excuse me ma'am), *monsieur* (sir), or *mademoiselle* (miss). Conversational tapes will help you get the pronunciation right.

Biking

Biking in France is wonderful, because when you get off the main roads, there are hundreds of scenic, untrafficked town roads and also paved farmers' paths.

PARIS

The magnificent architecture, stunning setting, and sophisticated atmosphere have inspired artists and writers for centuries.

Be sure to stroll along the famous broad avenues and use the metro (underground rapid transit) to get around. Metro stops for the following sights are indicated in parentheses. Highlights include:

Left Bank

- The Ile de la Cite. Here royal and ecclesiastical power once resided.

- Notre Dame. View the magnificent stained glass windows and impressive Gothic architecture. Climb to the top of the west facade for a wonderful view.

- The Latin quarter and Luxembourg Gardens.

- The Pantheon. View Paris from its colonnaded dome.

(For all of the above use metro stop Cite or Saint Michael.)

- Musee d'Orsay. It houses a famous collection of Impressionist, Post impressionist, and Nouveau Art in a spectacular setting. (Musee d'Orsay)

- Musee Rodin. Elegantly houses the famous sculpturer's work. (Metro Varenne)

- Eiffel Tower. (Metro Champ de Mars or Tour Eiffel)

- The Louvre Museum. One of the world's most famous art museums and home to da Vinci's Mona Lisa.

- Musee de l'Orangerie. Impressionist art. (metro Concorde)

- A walk down the Champs Elysees to see the Arc de Triomphe, Place de Concorde and the Jardin des Tuileries.

- Center Georges Pompidou. Has outstanding temporary exhibitions. (metro Rambuteau)

- Musee Picasso (metro Saint Sabastien)

- Opera Garnier, Paris' renown opera house.

- Montmartre. Area where the Moulin Rouge and Sacre Coeur are located. (metro Lamark Caulaincourt)

The metro system is excellent. Even if you are camping outside of town, it easy to catch a bus or train to take you to the nearest metro stop. This is an experience in itself. As on all mass transit systems, you get a look at everyday people doing everyday things. When taking the bus, have the camping place office write down the name of your destination stop and the name of your return stop. Show the name to a fellow passenger and ask them to tell you when to get off.

Camping places

- Western side of the Bois de Boulogne, off the Paris Ring road (Blvd. Peripherique), exit Porte Maillot, Bois de Boulogne; signs are posted from here: Camping du Bois de Boulogne. A camp shuttle bus takes and picks up campers from the Porte Maillot metro station in the morning and evening! This is a very popular camping place, so get here early.

- Southeast of Paris, near Bois de Vincennes, off the Paris Ring road A4 (Blvd. Peripherique), exit Porte Vincennes in the direction of Joinville; signs are posted after you cross the Marne River: Camping du Tremblay, close to the metro

- In Neuilly-sur-Marne, off N34 from Blvd. Peripherique or A4, in the direction of Vincennes at Neuilly-sur-Marne; signs are posted from the intersection of the River Marne and the Chelles canal: Muncipal Camping La Haute, near metro stop Neuilly Plaisance

- Farther away from the city, northwest of Paris, off the A13 or Paris-Rouen onto N308 to Maison-Laffite: Camping Maisons-Laffitte, close to train to Paris

GIVERNY

This small village just outside of Paris is where Monet had his home and gardens. There is a camping place behind the hostel: Auberge de Jeunesse.

Loire Valley

Situated between Brittany and Paris, this lovely area is where the wealthy and royal built lavish country homes during the sixteenth and seventeenth centuries. Biking is easy on the flat land, and rental bikes are readily available.

ORLEANS

Liberated by Joan of Arc in the fifthteenth century, Orleans has a lovely ambiance as well as some interesting museums and parks.

Camping places

- In Roche Aux Fees, on the Bois road along the River Loire: Camping St. Jean de la Ruelle, at Rue de la Roche
- In Olivet, between the River Loire and the River Loiret: Camping Muncipal Olivet, at rue du Pont-Bouchet

Tourist office

Next to the shopping center by the train station on pl. Albert

BLOIS

Some of the most outstanding chateaus, are close to Blois, a city that retains a medieval atmosphere.

Camping place

• Just east of the train station, on the south bank of the River Loire, near the helistation (heliport) and Pont Charles de Gaulle bridge: Camping Municipal La Boire, Blvd. du Docteur Alexis Carrel

Tourist office

In the outbuilding of the Chateaux de Blois, pavilion of Anne de Bretagne, at 3 av. Jean Laigret

Food market

Marche Couvert Halle Louis X11, Quai de L'Abbe Gregoire, open mornings and afternoons, closed Sundays and Mondays

Camping place

• Southwest of Chambord on D33: Camping Huisseau-sur-Cosson, at 6 Rue de Chatillonand on the Route de Chambord

Covered food markets, or _Les Halles,_ are in parentheses

• In Bracieux: Camping des Chateaux

• Near Chaumont, off the bridge on the south bank of the Loire: Camping Grosse Greve

• Near Amboise, across from the chateaus on the Ile d'Or

• Near Tours, many of them by the chateaus and the Loire (Les Halles—west of Rue Nationale at the Place Gaston Pailou, Monday through Saturday)

• Near Chenonceaux, close to the chateaus on the left side of the entrance of Chateauroux to Stade General Leclerc: Camping Municipal la Piscine, on rue Guintefol

• Near Azay-le-Rideau, across from the chateau on the Indre River

• Near Chinon, off RN 749, across the river at Ile Auger

• Near Angers, next to Centre d'Accueil (Les Halles—behind the cathedral at rue Plantagenet, Tuesday through Saturday)

Burgundy and Rhone Valley Area

A graceful region filled with medieval architecture, Burgundy and the Rhone valley feature hillsides dotted with small vineyards, villages, and fascinating museums.

DIJON This university town has an outstanding vielle ville.

Camping places
- Just west of the train station, behind Hospital des Chartreux
- Camping du Lac, 3 Blvd Chanoine; on a beautiful lake

Tourist office Place Darcy

Food markets Les Halles is in a nineteenth-century covered market, just north of Rue de la Liberte, Tuesday, Friday, and Saturday mornings. The Geant Casino is an extra-nice supermarket on bd. Clemenceau.

BEAUNE Beaune's fine architecture, wine, treasures, and vielle ville embrace what is the soul of France. Wine routes are on softly rolling hillsides and are great for biking. See the Hotel-Dieu, a fifthteenth-century hospital with unusual architecture.

Camping place
- Close to the center of town, off rue du Faubourg St. Nicholas (N74 to Dijon), before the bridge over the autoroute: Les Cent Vignes, 10 Rue Dubois

Tourist office Rue de l'Hotel-Dieu

Food market Les Halles at pl. Carnot, Saturday mornings

Camping place
- Across Pont de la Levee on the right: Camping Muncipal St. Vital

LYON This cosmopolitan city boasts dynamic museums, cultural life, excellent cuisine, and a well-preserved vielle ville.

Camping place
- In Dardilly, east of Lyon: Camping Municipal Porte de Lyon

Tourist office Southeast corner of Place Bellecour

Food markets	• Les Halles at 102 Cours Layfayetter, Tuesday through Saturday mornings
	• Street markets at Quai St. Antoine, Tuesday through Saturday mornings
	• bd. de la Croix Rousse (on the Rhone), Tuesday through Saturday mornings

French Alps

Majestic snow-covered peaks rising from rich farmlands give this area one of the world's most awe-inspiring sights.

GRENOBLE	This university town is at the edge of the French Alps, making it popular with sports enthusiasts from around the world.
Camping place	• In Seyssins, southwest corner of Grenoble, one block west of the Drac River: Camping Les Trois Pucelles, 58 Rue des Allobroges
Tourist office	Center of town, 14 rue de la Republique
Food markets	• Les Halles, near tourist office, Tuesday through Saturday mornings
	• Street market, Pl. St. Bruno near train station, west of the tracks; Monday through Saturday mornings.
CHAMONIX	This town is the most regal in the French Alps.
Camping places	• Near base of Aiguille du Midi telepherique: L'Ile des Barrats
	• Just south of Chamonix in Les Bossons, on the Route des Tissieres: Camping Les Deux Glaciers
	• In Les Pelerins, near turnoff to Mont Blanc Tunnel to Italy: Camping Les Arolles, 281 Chemin du Cry
	• In Argentiere, close to the train station: Camping Glacier d'Argentiere, 58 Chemin des Moilettes
Tourist office	Pl. du Triangle

Food market	• Street markets: pl. du Mont Blanc, Saturday mornings
	• Chamonix Sud (near foot of Aiguille du Midi telepherique), Tuesday mornings

Provence

Here the weather is bright and sunny much of the year. The extraordinary light and scenic countryside of this area attracted artists Van Gogh, Cezanne, and Picasso.

AVIGNON

A walled city with wonderful art museums, Avignon has a well-preserved vielle ville and the Palais des Papes, a huge medieval palace where the popes and their retinues lived.

Camping place

• On Ile de la Barthelasse, just north of Pont Edouard Daladier: Camping Bagatelle and Camping Municipal St.-Benezet

Tourist office

Three blocks from the train station, straight through Porte de la Republique onto Cours Jean Jaures, 150 meters up on the right, at 41 Cours Jean Jaures

Food markets

• Les Halles, is at Pl. Pie, Tuesday through Saturday mornings

• Street markets, outside the city walls near porte St. Michel, Saturday and Sunday mornings, and Codec at rue de la Republique, Monday through Friday mornings.

ARLES

Home to Van Gogh and Picasso, Arles is a lovely Provençal town with magnificent historic ruins. The wild life of Camargue is close by.

Camping places

• Close to Pont de Crau: Camping City, 67 route de Crau

• Just outside of Arles, N453, at Rapheles-les-Arles: La Bienheureuse

Tourist office

In esplanade Charles de Gaulle at Bd. des Lices across from the Jardin d'Ete

Food markets

Street markets at Bd. Emile Courbes, Wednesday mornings, and Bd. des Lices, Saturday mornings

AIX EN PROVENCE

Considered the gastronomic and cultural apex of Provence, this town is the oldest Roman settlement in France and birthplace of Cezanne.

Camping places

- Near the center of town, close to Pont des Trois Sautets, on the Rte de Nice: Arc-en-Ciel and Chantecler

Tourist office

At 2 Pl. du General de Gaulle

Food markets

Street market at Pl. de Verdun, Tuesday, Thursday, and Saturday mornings

Cote d'Azur

The French Riviera, or Cote d'Azur, stretches along the Mediterranean coast from Toulon to Menton. Look for the quieter stretches outside large towns, and avoid the area during July and August.

Camping places

- In St.-Tropez, route de Pampelonne, behind Pampelonne beach: La Croix du Sud and Kon Tiki; toward L'Escalet: Les Tournels

- In Grimaud, in Mediterranean village of La Garde-Freinet: Camping municipal St.-Eloi
- In St.-Rapael and Frejus on Camp-Long, route to Cannes from St.-Raphael: Royal Camping
- In Cannes in Ranguin, just west of Cannes, off the D9 towards Pergomes: Le Grande Saule, 24-26 Bd. de la Frayere, or Ranch-Camping, chemin St.-Joseph
- In Cannes, La Bocca, western suburb of Cannes, 67 av Maurice-Chevalier, or Aire Naturelle Clos St.-Hubert

Tourist office Next to the vieux (old) port in the Palais des Festivals, 1 Bd. de la Croisette

Food markets Street markets at pl. Gambetta and rue Forville, Tuesday through Saturday mornings

Camping place in Nice
- In Beausoleil, by rue Moyenne Corniche, Quartier Fondivine, Point Accueil: Jeunes de Beausoleil (very small but popular; arrive early)

Tourist office Near the casino, 2A, Bd. des Moulins

Camping places in Menton
- On route des Ciappes de Castellar: Camping St.-Michel
- Just west of the train station at 67 Vallee de Gorbio: Camping Fleur de Mai.

Tourist office In the Palais d'Europe, 8 Av. Boyer

Food market Les Halles across from Hotel d'Ville, Tuesday through Sunday, mornings

Bordeaux Region

Bordeaux is a large industrial city. Stay in one of the small towns with a medieval history, and go into Bordeaux for just the day or evening.

Tourist office Close to the Grand Theatre and Monument des Girondins, at 12 Cours du 30 Juillet

Camping places	• In Gradignan: Camping Beausoliel
	• In Villenave d'Ornon, close to Pont-de-laye-Maye: Camping Les Gravieres
	• In Rochelle, many along the Ile de Re (an island with sandy beaches), expensive toll bridge connects Rochelle with Ile de Re
	• In Arcrachon (a popular seaside resort), on allee de la Galaxie: Camping les Abatilles
	• In Plya-sur-Mer: Camping de la Dune

Basque Country

The Basque coast has beautiful sandy beaches and waves that attract world-class surfers. The vielle ville of St. Jean-de-Pied-de-Port is notable, and hiking and skiing are good in Foret d'Iraty.

BAYONNE	Stroll down Rue du Port Neuf to the oldest port in town and visit the Cathedrale Sainte Marie. Taste Izarra, a liqueur made from local herbs at Distillerie de la Cote Basque.
Tourist office	In Grand Bayonne, at Pl. de la Liberte in the Hotel de Ville, under the arcade on the side facing the river
Food market	In Grand Bayonne, on Nive River, mornings Tuesday–Saturday.
Camping places	• In Anglet, close to the hostel Auberge de Jeunesse: Camping de Fontaine Laborde
	• Close to Route de Bouney: Camping de La Chambre d'Amour
	• North of Anglet, on RN117, behind St. Espirit: Camping de la Cheneraie
BIARRITZ	Biarritz attracts sophisticates and surfers alike.
Tourist office	On the Square d'Ixelles, one block east of Ave Eduard V11
Food market	Marche Municipal at rue des Halles every morning

Camping places	• Close to Milady Beach: Camping Biarritz, 28 rue d'harcet
	• Close to the train station, quartier de Negresse, on Av. Kennedy: Camping Muncipal

Gascogne

Some of the most striking scenery in France is in this region: it has the snow-topped Pyrénées, pine-covered mountain slopes, and the pilgrimage site at Lourdes.

LOURDES

This sacred site is the second most visited city in France. Be prepared for large numbers of elderly and ailing persons. Visit as a day trip from Pau or Cauterets.

CAUTERETS

Thirty kilometers from Lourdes, this town is set right on the edge of the magnificent Parc National des Pyrénées and is the perfect base for hiking.

Tourist office

At the Maison du Parc Pl. du la Gare

Food markets

• Les Halles, in the center of town, daily

• Street market at Pl. du la Gare, Thursday and Friday mornings

Camping places

• Several are on the road from Lourdes.

Alsace-Lorraine

This area consists of rolling hillsides covered with vineyards in between small Bavarian/French towns with lovely gardens and window boxes overflowing with geraniums.

STRASBOURG

This city is considered the cosmopolitan center of Alsace. Tourists come to experience the lovely vielle ville of old Alsatian homes, narrow canals, and shops called La Petite France.

Tourist offices	Opposite the train station at Place de la Gare and also at Place de la Cathedrale
Camping places	• Just west of the city center, close to hostel Auberge de Jeunesse: Camping de la Montagne Verte, 2 rue Robert-Forrer
Food market	Street market, Pl. de Bordeaux, Tuesday through Saturday mornings

COLMAR   A beautifully kept small town, Colmar is 75 kilometers south of Strasbourg on the Route du Vin.

Camping place	• Out of Colmar, across the Ill River, on Rte. de Neuf Brisach RN415: Camping de L'Ill
Tourist office	Across from the Unterlinden Museum, 4 rue des Unterlinden
Food market	Street market, Pl. de l'Ancienne Duoane, Thursday mornings, and Pl. St. Joseph, Saturday mornings

NANCY   This university town has a well-restored baroque vielle ville. Close by in the Valley of the Vosges Mountains is the scenic town of Vittel.

Camping place	• On the RN74 towards Dijon: Camping de Brabrois
Tourist office	Close to Triumphal Arch, 14 Pl. Stanislas
Food market	Street market, Eglise St.-Sebastien, Monday through Saturday

Normandy

Situated on the rugged Atlantic coast, this region is home to the famous abbey of Saint Michel, the historic town of Rouen, and the D-Day landing beaches. It is famous for its calvados, camembert, and crepes.

Camping place	• Close to Rouen, in Deville-les-Rouen: Camping Municipal de Deville, at rue Jules Ferry

Tourist office	Opposite the cathedral, at 25 Pl. de la Cathedrale
Food market	Les Halles, at Pl. du Vieux March
BAYEUX	Close to the D-Day landings.
Camping places	• Close to RN13; follow rue Genas Duhomme to Av. de la Valle des Pres: Camping Municipal • In Etreham near Port-en-Bessin: Camping Reine Mathilde
Tourist office	Close to the cathedral in a fourteenth-century wooden building; from cathedral turn right onto Bienvenue, which becomes rue des Cuisiniers
MONT ST.-MICHEL	The magnificent abbey rises out of the water at this spot for an unforgettable sight. Visit in the morning before the tour buses arrive.
Camping places	• On D976, road to Pontorson: Camping St.-Michel, Rte. du Mont St.-Michel, and several more down this same road
Tourist office	Behind the stone wall on the left as you enter the walled city

Britagne

In this region of rough countryside and coast, indigenous traditions and language can still be experienced. It is a popular area for bicycling.

QUIMPER	Retaining its Breton architecture and ambiance, this city is considered to be the cultural center of Britagne. North of Quimper the land is flat and easy for biking.
Camping places	• Just west of the old city, in the Bois Seminaire next to the hostel: Camping Municipal, Av. des Oiseaux • Also on route de Benodet: Orangerie de Lannion.

Food market	Les Halles, off rue Kereon on rue St. Francois, Monday through Saturday
Tourist office	Off Pl. de Resistance; follow Av. de la Gare from train station, which becomes Bd. Dupleix, until you reach Pl. de la Resistance

CONCARNEAU   This unpretentious port town has lovely beaches.

Camping places
- Just out of town, near Plage des Sables Blancs: Camping Lanadan, and Camping du Dorlett
- Southeast of the Ville Close: Camping Moulin, at 49 Rue de Tregunc

Tourist office   Just north of the west gate to the Ville Close, on Quai d'Aiguillon

SAINT MALO   This walled city has nice beaches with very high tide variations.

Camping place
- In St.-Sevan near the promenade de la Corniche next to the Fort de la Cite: Camping de la Cite d'Aleth

Do not camp on the beach. What looks like a deserted sandy beach can be under water just hours later.

Tourist office   Near the entrance to the old city on Esplande St.-Vicent

Food markets
- Behind the Eglise Notre Dame-des-Greves, Monday, Thursday, and Saturday mornings
- At the Marche Aux Legumes, Tuesday and Friday mornings
- In Parame on Pl. du Prieure, Wednesday and Saturday mornings

French

Bonjour

Hello

S'il vous plait, ou est _____?

Please, where is _____?

Est-ce que vous pouvez l'ecrive.

Could you write it down.

Allez tout droit _____ (meters/kilometers) au _____ (regardez Liste Je Comprends).

Go straight ahead _____ (meters/kilometers) to _____ (look at List I Understand).

Premier tournez _____ (a droite/a gauche) allez _____ (meters/kilometers) au _____ (regardez Liste Je Comprends).

First turn _____ (right/left) go _____ (meters/kilometers) to _____ (look at List I Understand).

Prochain tournez _____ (a droite/a gauche) allez _____ (meters/kilometers) au _____ (regardez Liste Je Comprends).

Next turn _____ (right/left) go _____ (meters/kilometers) to _____ (look at List I Understand).

Combien de temps faut-il pour aller?_____ (minutes/heures)

How long will it take? _____ (minutes/hours)

Merci beaucoup

Thank you

List I Understand	Liste Je Comprends
corner	coin
stop sign	arret enseigne
traffic light	arret lumiere
exit	sortie
road	route/chemin
street	rue/chaussee
highway	autostrata
large	grand
small	petite
far	loin
near	pres
bridge	pont
river	riviere
river bank	quai
woods	foret
lake	lac
sea	mer
village	village
town	ville
city	cite
house	maison
train station	Gare SNCF
bus stop	arret d'autobus
red	rouge
green	verde
blue	bleu
yellow	jaune
white	blanc
black	noir
market place	marche
supermarket	supermarche
gas station	essence
square	place
main square	place centrale
castle	chateau
cathedral	cathedrale
church	eglise
camping place	camping
old town	vielle
beach	plage

Germany

A beautifully manicured country, Germany is well organized and interesting. Great rivers, famous museums and art galleries, dramatic castles, well-restored aldstadts (old towns), and wonderful hiking and biking trails all make it an easy country to enjoy.

Best time to go   April through October will be warmer and sunnier. But even in summer be ready for cool rainy days in between warm, sunny days.

Camping places   This is a wonderful country for camping. There is an abundance of clean, well-run camping places with green grass, trees, and flowers.

Driving   Because of the excellent maps, roadways, and road signs, this is one of the easier countries for driving. Aldstadt signs direct you to the old town.

Food markets   Open markets aren't as common here as they are in Italy and France. However the grocery stores and supermarkets are well stocked.

Tourist office   Known as DZT, the tourist offices are efficiently run and there will be a staff person who speaks English. They are often located close to or inside the train station.

Shop hours   Stores are usually open from 9 A.M. to 6 P.M. Smaller stores are often closed on Saturday afternoons and Sundays.

Eating out   The local cuisine is hardy and can be reasonably priced. Ethnic restaurants are plentiful. A gratuity is included in the bill, but it's nice to add in a little extra if the service has been good.

Bavaria

The countryside here is lush and beautiful, with medieval castles, scenic lakes, and dramatic mountains. Lovely little villages are set in among the gorges.

MUNICH

Englischer Garten is one of the largest city parks in Europe. It is very popular with the locals and a good place for people watching and bike riding.

In this city of outstanding museums, some of the most famous are:

- The Deutsch Museum. World's largest museum of science and technology, and should not be missed.
- The Residenz. It was once the palace of the Bavarian rulers.
- Pinakothck. This mammoth art museum is outstanding.

Camping places

- Southwest of city center: Campingplatz Thalkirchen, Zentral-landstrasse 49
- Toward Stuttgart: Waldcamping Obermenzing and Langwielder See
- In the Romantic Road area, in the town of Detwang: Camping Tauber-Idyll

Tourist office

At the Hauptbahnhof, or train station, south entrance by track 11. A great biking map called *Radl-Touren*, showing all the bike paths through the parks and the pedestrian area can be picked up here. A brochure on the *Romantische Strasse*, a scenic road outside of Munich that links picturesque villages from Wurzburg to Fussen, is also available here.

Food market

Just south of Marienplatz, Viktualienmarket

NUREMBERG

This university town has a well-restored aldstadt.

Camping place

- Southeast of city center off the B4 Ring Road, in Volspark near the Stadium: Campingplatz Am Stadion, Hans Kalbstrasse 56

Bavarian Alps

Here you are transported into the land of Heidi.

GARMISCH-PARTENKIRCHEN King Ludwig II's lavish palace here is a popular tourist attraction. The alpine lakes are almost unbelievably beautiful. Cable cars take you to the top of the Alps, where you can enjoy the view or hike down. There are saunas, steam baths, and tours of salt mines.

Camping places
- Close to Eibsee, along B4: Zugspitze; others in nearby towns
- In Konigasse, Grafenlehen and Mulleiten

Tourist office In Garmisch-Partenkirchen, at Richard Strausse Platz I

Bavarian Forest
(Bayerischer Wald)

The largest continuous forest area in Europe, the Bavarian Forest is an excellent hiking area.

Camping place   • In Zwiesel, near the sports center: Azur Camping

Baden-Württemberg

Popular with tourists, this area encompasses the Bavarian Forest, the beautiful lake Bodensee (Lake Constance), the picturesque town of Heidelberg, and the famous health spa Baden-Baden.

STUTTGART   This city is the industrial center for the area. Both Mercedes Benz and Porsche have museums and factories here.

Camping place   • By the river: Campingplatz Stuttgart, at Mercedestrasse 40

Tourist office   Outside the Hauptbahnhof, daily

BADEN-BADEN   This health spa attracts the wealthy.

Camping place   • In Buhl-Oberbruch: Campingplatz Adam

HEIDELBERG   The huge castle and Bavarian ambiance of this exquisite medieval town draw a considerable number of tourists. It is best avoided during July and August.

Camping place   • On the river, just outside the city: Camping Haide

Black Forest (Schwarzwald)

The Black Forest is named for its denseness. Of special interest are Mummelsee, a small, deep lake steeped in folklore, and the huge marketplace in Freudenstadtand. The area's small villages craft cuckoo clocks.

Camping places
- On the Schluchsee Wolfsgrund, outside of Freudenstadt: Camping Langenwald
- Near Bad Rippoldsau-schapbach, in the Black Forest: Schwarzwald-Camping-Alisehof
- In Freiburg: Camping Hirzberg, at Kartauserstrasse 99 North of Freiburg: Camping Breisgau

Lake Constance (Bodensee)

A popular lake resort because of its access into Switzerland and Austria, Lake Constance is a good cycling area.

Camping places
- East of Meersburg: Camping Hagnau
- In Uhldingen-Seeperle: Camping Seeperle
- Southeast of Lindau: Campingplatz Lindau-Zech

Danube River Area

The Danube is one of the greatest rivers in Europe. An excellent cycling path runs along the river from Ulm to Passau and into Austria.

Camping places
- In Regensberg: Campingplatz, am Weinweg 40
- In Passau: Zeltplatz, at Halserstrasse 34

Rhineland

Less heavily populated because of its rugged topography, Rhineland has deep river valleys, quaint towns, and vineyards producing grapes for the famous Moselle wine.

Camping places   Considerable number dot this area. Here are some:

- In Cochem, on the river, at the downstream end of town: Cochem Muncipal Campsite, on Stadionstrasse
- In Cochem, up the hill a bit: Jugenherberge
- In Koblenz, at the confluence of the Moselle and Danube Rivers, across from the Deutsches Eck Park, at the northeast corner of the city: Rhein Mosel
- In Wehlen, near Bernkastel-Kues: Camping Schenk
- In Traben-Trarbach: Rissbach, at Rissbacherstrasse 170
- In Bacharach, on the river at the southern end of town: Sonnenstrand
- In St. Goarshausen, on the cliff: Auf Der Loreley.

Tourist office
- In Koblenz, opposite the train station in a small round building in the bus station area
- In Mainz, down from the Bahnhof, on the corner of Bahnhofstrasse and Parcusstrasse

FRANKFURT   This large city has many interesting museums, a small but outstanding zoo, an extensive botanical garden, and popular apple wine taverns.

Camping place
- Northwest of city center in Heddernheim District: Heddernheim, at An der Sandelmuhle 35

Tourist office
- North of Hauptbahnhof, at Neethovenstrasse 69
- In the main train station at track 24
- In city, at Romerberg 27, northwest corner of the square

COLOGNE

The site of a magnificent cathedral and the famous Dom, this is also a good cycling city.

Camping places

- In Poll, 5 km southwest of city center: Municipal Camping Cologne-Poll, on Weidenweg
- In Cologne-Rodenkirchen, south of Poll: Camping Berger, at Uferstrasse 53a
- In Dunnwald, 15 km from Cologne: Camping Waldbad

Tourist office

Opposite the Dom entrance, at Unter Fettenhennen 19

Open market

At Alter Market, on Fridays; others during the week (Check with the tourist office.)

German

Guten tag

Hello

Bitte, wo ist _____?

Please, where is _____?

Konnen sie es bitte aufschreiben.

Could you please write it down.

Gehen Sie geradeaus _____ (meters/kilometers) zu _____ (sehen Liste Ich Verstehe).

Go straight ahead _____ (meters/kilometers) to _____ (show me List I Understand).

Biegen Sie _____ (rechts/links) gehen _____ (meters/kilometers) zu _____ (sehen Liste Ich Verstehe).

Turn _____ (right/left) go _____ (meters/kilometers) to _____ (see List I Understand).

Nachste biegen _____ (rechts/links) gehen _____ (meters/ kilometers) zu _____ (sehen Liste Ich Verstehe).

Next turn _____ (right/left) go _____ (meters/kilometers) to _____ (see List I Understand).

Wie weit ist? _____ (minutes/stundes)

How long will it take? _____ (minutes/hours)

Danke

Thank you

List I Understand	Liste Ich Verstehe
corner	ecke
stop sign	stop zeichen
traffic light	stop signal
exit	ausgang
road/street	strade
highway	autostrada
large	gross
small	klein
far	weit
near	nahe
bridge	brucke
river	flub
woods	wald
lake	see
sea	mer
harbor	hafen
village	ort
town/city	stadt
house	haus
train station	bahnhof
bus stop	bushaltestelle
red	rot
green	grun
blue	blau
yellow	geld
white	weiss
black	schwarz
market place	marketplatz
supermarket	supermarket
gas station	benzin
square	platz
main square	haupplatz
castle	schloss
cathedral	Dom
church	kirche
camping place	campingplatz
old town	alstadt
museum	museum

Greece

Ghosts of ancient times, the smell of lavender, and quiet fishing villages have drawn visitors here for centuries. Since it is also the birthplace of Western civilization, visitors also come here to absorb the roots of philosophy, the arts, and the sciences.

Best time to go

April through May and September through October are ideal for visiting. The summers are quite hot and crowded with tourists. Go to the archaeological sites early or late when they are quieter.

Museums and archaeological sites

There is so much to see. Go to the museum first for information about the archaeological site. Keep your ticket so that you can take a break, have lunch or a snack, and then return. Sunset and sunrise photos and experiences can be especially memorable.

Tourist offices

Known as EOT, they are usually at the main plaza. Camping in Greece, a brochure, is available.

Camping places

Camping places are plentiful, particularly close to beaches. When you get to the general area where you know there is a camping place, check the right-hand side of the road very carefully for a camping sign. Camp signs are generally posted from the center of town, and there might be only one or two signs to direct you. Often there will be a kilometer indication. Check your odometer and use this for a general guide. Shower water is often solar heated, so shower after the water has time to heat up and before it cools down.

Driving

Greek drivers are aggressive so you need to be, too. Secondary roads are good, but have only two lanes. Small towns have narrow streets and are difficult for a wide camper van to maneuver. Many signs are only in Greek, particularly away from the main tourist areas.

Special maps are needed

You'll need a map that has the Greek spellings, too. Order these early from your travel bookstore and take them with you to Greece. Stop your vehicle in front of the sign and check, very carefully, the spelling of the words to make sure you are going in the right direction.

Food markets   Street markets are plentiful. Once or twice a week, larger open markets called Laiki Agora are held. It is wise to purchase bread and meat in the morning. Meat isn't always displayed. Ask if meat is available. Use the fill-in forms to help you get what you want.

Eating out   Menus here reflect the interesting combination of Greek and Turkish cuisine. A service charge is included, but leave a little extra if the service has been good.

ATHENS   To get the spirit of the ancient and the somewhat raucous present:

- See the Acropolis early in the morning and again at sunset.
- Investigate the ancient Agora.
- Rest in a cafe and absorb the atmosphere of the Plaka.
- See the National Archaeological Museum, which houses the world's largest collection of Greek antiquities.

Camping places
- West of the city, east of Dafni on the Athine-Korinthos highway: Camping Athens
- West of the city, on the Athine-Korinthos highway, near the Dafni Monastery and next to an amusement park: Camping Dafni
- In Nea Kiffissia, north of Athens on the highway to Larissa: Camping Acropolis
- South of Athens, near Glifada airport, on the coast road to Voula: Edt Camping Voula

Take public transportation to the old city center.

Tourist office   On the Syntagma (Athen's main square), the National Bank and the General Bank have EOT desks that dispense maps, bus timetables, and This Week in Athens.

Food markets (Laki Agora)
- Huge indoor market, in Monastiraki area on Athinas
- Close to the train station on Psarson on Wednesdays
- In the Mets and Pangrati areas and on Arhimidous; on Fridays
- Around the train station at Alkamenous, on Saturdays

These same areas have bakeries, fish and butcher shops, and grocers and greengrocers.

DELPHI

Sunset and sunrise on the slopes of Mt. Parnassos, overlooking the Gulf of Corinth, are the best times to enjoy Delphi's lovely temples, well-preserved amphitheater, intriguing Castella springs, and excellent museum. Camp close by so you can absorb its wonder.

Camping places

- Just west of Delphi: Apolonos Camping, swimming pool, fabulous view
- Southwest of Delphi, on Itea Road: Delphi Camping, swimming pool, wonderful view
- At the beach in Itea: Kparelis Camping and Ayannis Camping

Peloponnese

MYCENAE

A powerful kingdom for four hundred years, Mycenae is poetically known through Homer's epics.

Camping places	• In Mycenae Village: Camping Mycenae
	• West edge of Mycenae, close to the Corinth-Argos Road: Camping Atreus
	• At the beach, along the coast just south east of Nafplion, water sports equipment rental
	• On the spectacular coast southwest of Nafplion to Leonidio; further away but less touristy

EPIDAURUS   One of Greece's most famous sites, this is the home of Asklepios, god of medicine. The third century theater here is considered by many to be the best preserved building in ancient Greece.

Camping place   • West of the archaeological site, on the coast close to Palea Epidavros

OLYMPIA   The beautiful setting of the ruins of the ancient Olympic games, this is a very special place to be at sunrise and sunset.

Camping places   • Close to the center of the village, on the road to Krestens: Camping Diana and Camping Olympia; swimming pools
    • On the road to Pyros: Camping Alphios
    • On the beach, north and south of Olympia: many camping places

Tourist office   By bus stop at Praxitelous Kondili.

MYSTRA   Once a beautiful city; now the ruins spill down from Mt. Taygetos. Park at the top and work your way halfway down, then repark at the bottom and see the lower parts.

Camping places   • Just east of Mistra on the Mistra-Sparta Road
    • On the coast near Gythio, several

The Island of Crete

The largest of the islands, Crete is well known for its Minoan archaeological sites as well as its lovely beaches, mountains, and gorges.

IRAKLION

This is the capital of Crete and location of the important archaeological museum. Go to the museum before going out to Knossos.

Camping places

- On the beach, east of Iraklion, off the National Highway at Gouves: lots of campsites

KNOSSOS

Site of the Minoan culture of 1900 B.C.; the Knossos palace was painstakingly reconstructed.

PHAESTOS

The ruins here are second in importance to Knossos. There are wonderful vistas of the Mesara Plain and Mt. Ida.

Camping places

- On the south coast, in Matala, just back from the beach: Matala Community Camping
- On the south coast in Agia Galini, east of town on the beach, signs posted on the Iraklion-Agia Galini Road: Agias Galini Camping
- On the south coast in Plakias: Camping Apollonia; swimming pool

HANIA

This lovely old Venetian city has an especially wonderful waterfront and a covered food market dating from the turn of the century. Popular treks and mountain climbing start from this area.

Camping places

• On the beach, west of town: Hania Camping

SAMARIA GORGE

The largest gorge in Europe, this national park is popular with trekking tourists. From Xyloskalo the trail goes through the gorge down to the coast, exiting at Agia Roumeli. The walk takes about 4 to 6 hours. Wear hiking shoes, and bring water and lunch.

Note: To do this hike you need to arrange transportation. At the bus station in Hania, buy an early morning bus ticket to the top of the gorge (Omalas Plateau). On the day of your trek, leave your vehicle at the campsite and take a bus or taxi to the bus station. At the end of the hike get a ticket in Agia Roumeli for the ferry to Hora Sfakion, a short scenic ferry ride. At Hora Sfakion, buy a bus ticket back to Hania. The bus ride back is about a 1½-hour ride through spectacular countryside.

The Island of Rhodes

This is the largest inhabited medieval town in Europe. Its fortifications are the finest surviving. Walking through the winding streets you see a mixture of Latin, Byzantine, and Turkish architecture. The ruins of the ancient city of Lindos are also here. This is a good island for sunseekers vacationing in late fall.

Camping places

• On the beach at Faliraki and Lardos

Tourist office

West of Plateia Rimini on, the corner of Makariou and Papagou.

The Island of Tilos

Situated west of Rhodes, this unspoiled island has superb beaches. The terrain is less barren and rocky than some other islands. Camping is "freelance".

The Island of Kos

The site of an important Neolithic settlement as well as a flourishing Mycenaean city, this was the birthplace of Hippocrates, the father of medicine.

Camping place
- Eastern waterfront, signs posted from the port

The Island of Patmos

This is an important pilgrimage site for Christians, because St. John wrote the Apocalypse here.

Camping place
- Close to Skala at Meloi Beach, signs from the quay: Patmos Flower Camping

The Island of Samothrace

The dramatic landscape of this small island is impressive. It is the site of the Sanctuary of the Great Gods, the precursors of the Olympian gods. Beaches are rocky.

Camping places
- East of Kamariotisa, on the main road just beyond Loutra

The Island of Corfu

Considered by many to be the most beautiful of the Greek islands, Corfu's narrow streets, gardens, and two ancient fortresses give it a European feeling. It is heavily touristed.

Camping places
- Close to Corfu town on Kontokali Beach, next to the youth hostel
- On the north east coast there are several
- Western side of Corfu at Paleokastritsa
- Near Glyfada in the village Vatos

The Island of Zakynthos

Outstanding beaches and natural beauty make this a popular island. A guided trip to the Blue Caves should not be missed.

Camping place
- In Tsilivi: Zante Camping

The Island of Skiathos

Lovely beaches attract great numbers of tourists to this island.

Camping places
- West of Skiathos town, at Kolios Beach
- North coast, at Megalili, on Aselinos Beach

The Island of Mykonos

A beautiful island with its much photographed, brightly painted balconies, red-tiled roofs, and blooming bougainvillea. The island, which is busy with tourists, is also the gay capital of Greece.

Camping places
- On Paradise and Parage Beaches

The Island of Paros

This island is famous for its white marble, olive groves, vineyards, and old quarter.

Close by are:
- Naoussa, a relaxed fishing village with camping place.
- Valley of the Butterflies, in Pataloudes, just south of Paroikia (July–August).

Camping places
- Northern beach, close to the capital and port city of Paroikia: Camping Koula

- Just south of Paroiki: Parasporos Camping
- On Kreyos Beach, opposite the port: Krios Camping

The Island of Folegandros

This beautiful untouristy island has cultivated hills and pleasant fishing villages.

Camping place

- Close to Karavostassi, on Livadi Beach

The Island of Thira (Santorini)

Volcanic eruptions have made the landscape here extremely dramatic. The caldera, museum, Minoan excavations, and boat trips to Thirassia to see the volcanic activity are all interesting. Commercialism detracts from its charm.

Camping places

- Just east of Plateos Theotokopoulou, in Fira
- Kamari and Perissa Beaches, on the east coast
- At Kamari, just up from the main road: Kamari Camping
- At Perissa, on the beach Monolithos

Greek
(Pronunciation Only)

Ya-su

Hello

Paraka-lo, pu i-ne _____?

Please, where is _____?

Paraka-lo, ghrah-psteh to.

Please, could you write it down.

Pee-yeh-neh teh ee-see-ah _____ (meters/kilometers) sto _____ (dheek-steeh Leh-ksee Kah-tah-la-veh).

Go straight ahead _____ (meters/kilometers) to _____ (point to Words I Understand).

Protto (stree-psteh/ah-ree-steh-rah) _____ (meters/kilometers) sto _____ (dheek-steeh Leh-ksee Kah-tah-la-veh).

First go right/left _____ (meters/kilometers) to _____ (point to Words I Understand).

Eh-po-meh-no(stree-psteh/ah-ree-steh-rah) _____ (meters/kilometers) sto _____ (dheek-steeh Leh-ksee Kah-tah-la-veh).

Next (go right/left) _____ (meters/kilometers) to _____ (point to Words I Understand).

Po-see or-rah dhee-ahr-kee to tah-ksee-dhee? _____ (lehp-tahs/orrahs)

How long will it take? _____ (minutes/hours)

Ehf-khah-ree-sto

Thank you

Words I Understand	**Lehk-see Kah-tah-lah-veh-no**
intersection	stah-vro-dhro-mee
stop sign	stah-mah-tah see-mah
traffic light	stah-mah-tah eh-lah-fre-ess
exit	ehk-sod-hoss
road	dh-ro-moss
street	thro-moss
highway	kee-nee-to dh-ro-moss
large	meh-gha-loos
small	mee-kros
far	mah-kree-ah
near	kon-dah
bridge	yeh-fee-rah
river	po-tah-moss
woods	dhah-ss-o-ss
sea	thah-lah-ssah
harbor	lee-mah-nee
village	khor-ree-o
town/city	po-lee
house	spee-tee
train station	stah-mah-tah to-treh-no
bus stop	stah-mah-tah to leh off or reeo
red	ko-kee-noss
green	prah-see-noss
blue	bleh
yellow	kee-tree-noss
white	ah-spro-ss
black	mah-vross
market place	ah-ghor-rah
supermarket	supermarket
gas station	stah-th-moss vehn-zee-nee
square	plah-tee-ah
main square	kehn-dro plah-tee-ah
castle	kah-stro
church	eh-klee-see-ah
camping place	kah-tah-skee-nos-see
old town	pah-lee-ah po-lee
museum	moo-see-o
beach	para-li-ah
ruins	eh-ree-pee-o
building	to-ktee-ree-o

Hungary

A romantic country steeped in history, Hungary was home to Liszt and Bartok as well as to wonderful gypsy music and dance. It has been repeatedly invaded both because of its location in the center of eastern Europe and because the Danube River, an important water route, runs through it. The country offers castles, medieval villages, and colorful folklore. Musical entertainment is easy to find, and ticket prices are reasonable. Thermal baths are plentiful and fun to try. The Hungarians love horses; arrangements for riding can be made at the tourist office.

The countryside is a combination of gently rolling hills and flatlands. Bicycling is wonderful and opportunities for canoeing, kayaking and other sports abound.

Camping places

There are many good camping places in very scenic places.

Tourist offices

Ibusz offices are travel agents, but they also serve as tourist offices and dispense tourist information. Each usually has someone who speaks English. Museums are generally closed on Mondays and are sometimes free on Saturdays.

Bring your own maps and guide books from the United States.

Shop hours

Grocery stores are usually open from 7 A.M. to 7 P.M. on weekdays and on Saturday mornings.

Driving

Driving is easy because the roads are well marked and not heavily trafficked. Unleaded gas is harder to find than leaded 86 octane and 92 octane. Diesel is harder to find than regular gas. A green flashing light at an intersection means the same thing as a yellow flashing light in the United States.

Food markets

Grocery stores are located near the large housing developments. Food is good and prices are reasonable. Hungary is noted for its fine wines, produce, and meat.

BUDAPEST   Budapest is often called the Paris of Eastern Europe. The Danube meanders through this contemporary, sophisticated city, dividing it in two. Buda is on the hillside and is more historic. Pest is flatter and filled with shops and restaurants. Seven bridges span the Danube.

Interesting are:

- Castle Hill area. Get a map for a guided tour at the tourist office. It is like walking through an open-air museum.
- Margaret Island. Set in the middle of the Danube, this graceful garden area offers a wonderful respite from the city.
- Royal Palace. Houses the Museum of Fine Arts and has a fine collection of paintings and sculpture.
- National Museum. Houses artifacts and exhibits on Hungarian history from the period leading up to the Magyar conquest through contemporary times.
- Cog railway. Winds its way through wooded Buda to the top of the hill.
- A cruise on the Danube River. This is best in the evening, when you can view the city's castle, parliament, and citadella lit up.
- A side trip up to the Danube Bend, to Szentendre and Esztergom. To buy tickets and board for any cruise, go to the yellow ticket office on the river side of the left bank, just below the Duna Inter-Continental Hotel, at Vigado ter.
- Thermal baths. There are 140 thermal baths in Budapest alone. Gellert Baths has a large thermal swimming pool with beautiful mosaics covering its vaulted walls and is an easy bath for tourists enjoy. Located below the Gellert Hill, facing the Danube, you enter through the hotel of the same name. Remember that many people go to the thermal baths to treat ailments.

Camping places

- North of the city in Romaifuro: a large camping place; railway available to city center
- In the Buda Hills: Harshegy Camping; bus available to city center.
- Bottom of the Buda Hills at chairlift; Zugligeti; bus available to city center

Danube Bend Area

Because the Danube has been a major transportation route since prehistoric times, this area is steeped in history. No bridges cross the river here, so you need to take a ferry. If you drive, stay on the west bank as you leave Budapest going in the direction of Szentendre. The excursion boat from Budapest is a wonderful alternative way to visit this area.

SZENTENDRE

This is probably the most colorful of the towns along the river. You can see the castles of medieval kings and the seventeenth-century settlements of wealthy Serbian merchants. Today it is a thriving artists' colony.

Camping places

- On Pap Island, north of Szen, near the Danube riverboat landing, across the bridge from the Hotel Danubius

VISEGRAD

This historic city is located at the horseshoe bend of the river. Hungarian kings built a huge citadel on top of the hill, with a wall running down to another castle closer to the river. It has been excavated by archaeologists and now you can visit the ruins. It is a nice hike up to the citadel, where there is a marvelous view of the Danube. A thermal swimming pool is close by in Lepence.

Camping places

- North of the Nagy-Villam Tower, high on the hillside: Jurta Camping
- Behind the church with the green tower: a small camping place
- West of Visegard, at Domos, close to the riverboat landing and bus stop

ESZTERGOM

This is probably Hungary's most historically significant city. It is considered the cradle of Hungarian Christianity. Esztergom Cathedral was rebuilt in the 1800s. Its treasury is so rich that it is called the Vatican of Hungary. The remains of the Royal Palace are called the Varmuzeum, and parts have been painstakingly restored. From its hillside setting you get a wonderful view of the area.

Camping places

- Primas Island, on Nagy-Duna setany, south of old bridge: Gran-Tour s Camping.
- On road to Visegard: Vadvirag Camping

Western Trandanubia

Situated northwest of Balaton Lake, and bounded by the Danube and the Alps, this pretty area is dotted with picturesque, flower-filled villages.

SOPRON

The most historic city in this region, Sopron is also one of the best preserved, because, fortunately, it was never invaded by the Tartars or Turks.

Include in your sightseeing:

- A walk through the historic horseshoe-shaped and partially walled old village.
- Liszt Ferenc Museum. Located in a villa on the corner of Deak ter and Muzeum, this museum is for music lovers.
- Esterhazy Palace, the Versailles of Hungary. There are 126 baroque-style rooms and huge gardens. Haydn was once the court composer and conductor, a room is dedicated to him and his memorabilia. The palace is close by in Fertod, east of Sopron.

Camping place

- Just south of the railway station on Koszegi ut: Lover Camping place, close to the hotel by the same name

Balaton Lake

This area is known as the Riviera of Hungary. Being the largest freshwater lake in central and eastern Europe makes it very popular with vacationers from Hungary, Germany, and Austria. The warm, shallow water and sandy beaches attract families. On the northern side of the lake the beaches are pebbly. This side also has the finely restored castle at Keszthely and the famous Tihany Abbey—the site of Hungary's first Christian church. The whole area is dotted with vineyards and fruit orchards.

SIOFOK

Siofok is the largest and busiest beach town on the southeastern shore.

Camping place

- Golden Lake Camping, just one of many

BALATONFURED   The thermal waters of this quiet and elegant spa town attract many cardiac patients.

Camping place   • West end of Balatonfured, off highway 71 toward the lake, by Hotel Marina: FICC Rallying Camping

TIHANY   This town is on a peninsula that stretches into the lake. The most beautiful area around the lake, it has forests and is home to the famous Benedictine Tihany Abbey, where the crypt of King Andrew the First, dated 1060, is found.

KESZTHELY   • People come to Keszthely to see the Festetics Palace. It has 101 rooms. The library is particularly notable.
   • Close to Keszthely is Lake Gyogy, the second largest thermal lake in the world. Wooden catwalks make it easy to enjoy the thermal waters.

Camping places   • South of the railroad station, across from the tracks, along the lakeshore: Zalatour Camping
   • East edge of Keszthely, off highway 71 toward the lake: Castrum Camping

Southern Transdanubia

Situated close to Yugoslavia, this area is filled with forested hills.

PECS   A favorite Hungarian city for many, Pecs has a beautiful climate that is warmer and more Mediterranean than in other parts of Hungary. The area has attracted settlers for two thousand years. Many of the homes have red tile roofs, making it reminiscent of southern European countries. Because it is located on the southern slopes of the Mecsek hills, hiking is good. The city has a good archaeological museum as well as other interesting museums, churches, and summer cultural activities.

Camping places   • In the city center, at Felsoramhaz utca 72: Dozso Campsite
   • Near the zoo in the Mecsek Hills, follow the road to the TV tower: Mandulas Camping

Great Plain Puszta

Once similar to the American prairie, Puszta is now a major farming area. However, Hungarian cowboys and long-horned gray cattle can still be found.

KECSKEMET

The town is surrounded by fruit trees and vineyards. The great theater Katona is located here, and the town is the birthplace of composer Zoltan Kodaly.

Camping places

- Southwest side of Kecskemet, on the Sport utca
- West end of Kecskemet, off Kecskemet-Dunafoldvar Highway #52: Autoskemping

BUGAC

There are horse shows here every day in summer in Kiskunsay National Park.

Camping place

- Not far from the Bugac-Felso railroad station, next to the Bugacium Csarda restaurant

SZEGED

A city of boulevards and parks, Szeged is a major producer of paprika and salami. In July and August, a famous summer festival features first-rate opera, theater, and dance. The magnificent neo-Byzantine Votive Church is located here.

Camping places

- Next to Napfeny Panzio Hotel: Napfeny Panzio, On Dorozsmai ut 2
- In Ujszeged, near the strand: Partfurdo Camping, Kozepkikoto sor

DEBRECEN

Located close to Romania, this is a large industrial city. There have been settlements here since the Stone Age.

Notable are:

- Great Reformed Church. This is the largest Protestant church in Hungary.
- Deri Museum. The museum holds some Etruscan pieces as well as a notable collection of east-Asian artifacts, the most popular being the huge Ecce Hono painting by Munkacsy.

- Nagyerdo Forest Park. There is a zoo, a public swimming pool, boat rentals, and pleasant walking paths.
- Hortobagy National Park. Folklore programs feature the horsemen, shepherds, and gypsies.

Camping places
- In Nagyerdo Forest Park, close to the Thermod Hotel
- In Hortobagy, on the Debrecen-Fuzesabony Highway, near the National Park

Northern Hungary

Northern Hungary once guarded Budapest from northern invaders. In this densely forested area, featuring low hills and the ruins of medieval castles, both tokay and red wines of renown are produced.

EGER

This lovely old city is filled with baroque architecture. The Bull's Blood of Eger, a robust red wine, is produced here. Now a national monument, the Eger Castle ruins and its museum are interesting to visit. Thermal and Turkish baths are a relaxing diversion.

Camping place
- North of Eger, at Rakoczi utca 79: Autokemping

AGGTELEK NATIONAL PARK

Situated on the border, Aggtelek National Park has Hungary's largest and most scenic caves. Don't miss the Baradia Caves and the boat trip to an underground lake. Dress warmly and wear comfortable walking shoes for caving.

Camping place
- At the entrance to the National Park

TOKAJ

Known throughout the wine world for its fabulous tokay wine, Tokaj has produced wine since the eleventh century. The Wine Museum is worth a visit.

Camping place
- Southwest of Tokaj, near the Theiss River, on the Tokaj-Nyiregyhaza Highway #38.

Hungarian

Szia

Hello

Kerem, hol van _____?

Please, where is _____?

Kerem, ir ja le.

Write it down, please.

Elore megy _____ (meters/kilometers) hoz _____ (lat Jegyzek En Ertem).

Go straight ahead _____ (meters/kilometers) to _____ (see list I Understand).

Elso fordul _____ (jobb/ba) megy _____ (meters/kilometers) hoz _____ (lat Jegyzek En Ertem).

First turn _____ (right/left) go _____ (meters/kilometers) to the _____ (see list I Understand).

Kovetkezo fordul _____ (jobb/ba) megy _____ (meters/kilometers) hoz _____ (lat Jegyzek En Ertem).

Next turn _____ (right/left) go _____ (meters/kilometers) to _____ (see list I Understand).

Memnyi i deig tart a kirandulas? _____ (percs/oras)

How long will it take? _____ (minutes/hours)

Koszonom.

Thank you.

List I Understand	Liste En Ertem
corner	saroknal
intersection	keresztezes
stop sign	melgallas jel
traffic light	forgalom feny
exit	kijaret
road	ut
street	utca
highway	orszagut
large small	nagy
far	messze
near	kozeli
bridge	hid
river	folyo
woods	fa
lake	to
sea	tenger
harbor	kikoto
village	kozseg
town	kicsi varos
city	varos
house	haz
train station	vonat allomas
bus stop	autobusz mellgallas
red	piros
green	zold
blue	kek
yellow	sarga
white	feher
black	fekete
market place	vasar
grocery store	fuszer azlet
gas station	gaz allomas
square	negyzet
main square	fo negyzet
castle	kastely
cathedral	szekeseghaz
church	eghaz
camping place	tabor hely
old town	oreg varos

Italy

A wonderfully scenic country, Italy is filled with rolling hills planted with grapevines, wheat, and sunflowers. Old villas edged with majestic cypress trees, tiny hilltop villages and medieval towns seem to be everywhere. It is also home to excellent food and fabulous art.

Best time to go
April through June and September through October are prime times to visit. The weather is good then and, because there are fewer tourists, prices are lower. July and August should be avoided, because the country is crowded then with tourists.

Tourist offices
Tourist offices are called EPT, APT, or AAST.

Shop hours
Businesses usually open by 9 A.M. close around 1 P.M. for lunch, and reopen after 3 P.M. The Italians take lunch very seriously.

Camping places
Most camping places are open April through mid-October. You need to watch very closely on the right-hand side of the road as you come into the general area of a prospective camping place. Camping places often have only two posted road signs. Second-home campers are plentiful in the camping places here.

Driving
The toll on the autostradas is heavy, particularly for camper vans. Use the smaller roads when possible, as they are free and more scenic. Regular gas is called benzina; unleaded is called benzina senza piombo.

When visiting walled towns, look for parking just outside the walled center. Mark where you are on your city map and then note some buildings or signs that you will remember. Because walled cities have several entrances, it's easy to lose track of where you parked.

Eating out
Use your guidebook to find recommended restaurants and enjoy some of the wonderful food Italy offers. Make reservations if possible.

ROME
This ancient capital of an empire that spread throughout most of Europe and into northern Africa is fabulous for walking. It should be savored by wandering through the fascinating streets, over bridges, and into piazzas.

Don't drive your vehicle into the center of Rome. Find your campsite, then take public transportation into the city each day. (See "Using Public Transportation.") Dress appropriately for the whole day and early evening. Be aware that both men and women should not wear shorts or sleeveless tops in cathedrals.

Go to museums in the morning; many are closed in the afternoon. Relax in the afternoons by leisurely wandering through sights such as the Roman Forum, Palatine, and Coliseum.

Don't miss:

- The Vatican and its magnificent treasures.

- St. Peter's Cathedral and the vibrantly colored frescos by Michelangelo in the Sistine Chapel.

Camping places
- Just north of Rome, via Cassia 1216: Seven Hills, shuttle bus to city center.

- Off GRA (Rome's Ring Road) exit SS-6, via Flamina Nuova, 821: Flamingo

- Close to Vatican, off exit SS-1, exit Aurelia toward city center: Roma Camping; can be crowded

- Just north of city, direction Terni, off GRA (Rome's Ring Road), exit SS-3: Camping Tiber

- In the same area, SS-3 (via Flamina) toward Terni, exit Prima Porta: Roman River Camping

- Close to Leonardo da Vinci airport, near excavation at Ostia Antica: Capitol Camping

Food market
- Campo de Fiori, mornings except Sunday; huge

- Wholesale food market, at Via Ostiense, good for photographs

Umbria

Located in the green heart of Italy, this region is the home of Saint Francis of Assisi, thermal springs, Etruscan ruins, and verdant countryside—rolling hills, woods and streams.

PERGUGIA

This university town holds an impressive collection of medieval and Renaissance art.

Camping place

* In Colle dells Trinita, north west from town, on Via del Marcato: Camping Paradis D'Ete

Food market

At P.Europa and P.Mattecotti, Tuesday and Saturday mornings

Tourist office

In Palazzo dei Priori, at P.IV November

ASSISI

Popular with Italy's religious youth, this is the site of the Basilica di San Francesco.

Food market

At Via San Gabriele, Saturday mornings

Camping places

* Uphill in Fontemaggio, on the road to Etremo delle Carceri, ½ mile south east of town; part of the youth hostel (The access road is steep.)
* Just west of town, off SS 75 on SS 147: Camping Internazionale

GUBBIO	This picturesque town has winding medieval streets.
Tourist office	Off Corso Garibaldi, on Piazza Oderisi 6
Camping places	• South of town, on Highway 298
LAGO TRASIMENO	This is a placid lake with a reed-lined shore.
Camping places	• Camping places dot the whole lake.
VALSORDA	Large caves are in the mountains.
Camping places	• At Fornace, northeast of Gualdo: Rio Verde • In Caglioli: Plan Di Boccio

SPOLETO   Set on a hillside, this picturesque city is filled with graceful medieval charm.

Tourist office   At P.della Liberta 7

Food market   At Piazza del Mercato, Monday through Saturday mornings

Camping places
- In Spoleto, just off the main Terni/Spoleto Road, behind the church of San Pietro, downhill from Piazza Liberta: Camping Monteluco
- In Petrognano: Il Girasole

ORIVIETO   This Etruscan town is the site of the Duomo, one of the greatest gothic buildings in Italy.

Camping places
- On Lake Corbara, near Baschi: Camping Orvieto
- Close by at Lago di Piediluco and at Monte del sole
- In town, tents only: Agricampeggio Sossogna, Rocca Ripasena 61

Tuscany

Located in the heart of Italy, Tuscany, with its ancient walled towns, cypress trees, rolling hills, and vineyards, evokes the essence of Italy.

FLORENCE

Artistic genius was supported by the wealthy in Florence. Thus it flowered, leaving the incomparable heritage of the Italian Renaissance. Tourist sites are within a relatively small area, so walking is the way to go. Get an early start. Most of the museums are closed in the afternoons.

See as much as you can of:
- The Accademia
- Uffizi Gallery
- Pitti Palace
- Bargello Palace and National Museum
- Medici Chapel and Church of San Lorenzo

In the afternoons stroll through Ponte Vecchio, Duomo, Piazza della Signoria, and Palazzo Vecchio.

Food market

Mercato Centrale, in the historic area; a world-class covered market, mornings

Tourist office

APT Offices: via Tornabuoni, and Chiasso Baroncelli 19r (just off Piazza della Signoria)

Camping places	• Near Pl. Michelangelo, on the south side of the Arno, via le Michelangelo 80, set on the hillside overlooking the Arno River and the Duomo, close to the historic area; very crowded but worth it if you can get in (Check in early.)

Camping places

- Near Pl. Michelangelo, on the south side of the Arno, via le Michelangelo 80, set on the hillside overlooking the Arno River and the Duomo, close to the historic area; very crowded but worth it if you can get in (Check in early.)
- Northeast of city, on road to Fiesole, by the HI (hostel) : Villa Camerata, Viale A. Righi 2/4
- Just northeast of Fiesole, on a hill just north from Florence: Panoramico, via Peramonda 1, steep access road
- Just southwest of the city in Bottai, off A-1 Firenze-Rome Hwy exit Certose, near monastery: Camping International Firenze
- Halfway between Siena and Florence, on a hillside overlooking the Chianti region of Tuscany, north of Poggibonsi in Barberino Val d'Elsa: Camping Semifonte, Barberino Val d'elsa, via Cassia 71

CORTONA

This ancient hill town is located in the center of Tuscany.

Open markets

- At Piazza della Republica
- Agricultural fair and market, in Camucia, Mondays

SIENA

This gothic town exudes medieval atmosphere and beauty. The perfectly preserved, ancient hilltop village of San Gimignano is close by.

Open market

At P. del Duomo

Tourist office

AAST: Via di Citta

Camping places

- West of Siena, near Badesse on SS 2, Firenza/Siena: Camping Luxor Badesse
- 2 km north east of Siena: Campeggio Siena Colleverde, Strada di Scacciapen Sieri 47
- Just downhill from Porta San Gimignano in Santa Lucia
- In Monteriggioni, off road from Siena to Volterra: Siena/Tuscan Camping

VOLTERRA

This ancient town is set strikingly on a huge bluff.

Camping place

- In Balzo: Camping Le Balze, via Mandringa 15

MONTEPULCIANO   This wonderful small hill town is the highest in Tuscany. Its wine, olive oil, and pastries are well known. At Fattorie, wine and other products from the region's farms can be tasted.

Open market   At Porta al Prato, Thursdays

MONTALCINO   This classy Tuscan hill town is known for its Brunello wines. The magnificent Abbey di Sant'Antimo is close by.
There are sulfur springs, cascade, close by. To get to them, pass through the small town of Saturnia and its spa, go a bit further and stop when you see parked cars. The cascate has formed pools of hot sulfur water, like hot tubs, in the rocks that are fun to soak in.

Camping places   • Nearby, just north of Chiusi, on Lago di Chiusi: Pesce D'oro
    • In Sarteano, not far from Siena: Camping Della Piscine
    • Just north of sulphur springs, at Terme di Saturnia

LUCCA   This lovely walled city is in the middle of Tuscany's rich agricultural land.

Camping places   • Outside of Viareggio, in the area of Torre del Largo Puccini, there are several camping places.

PIZA   The site of the leaning tower at Campo dei Miracoli, this famous town also has a wonderful Duomo and Camposanto.

Camping places   • Just west of Campo dei Miracoli, directional signs from Piazza Manin: Campeggio Torte Pendente, Viale della Cascine 86
    • Near Marina di Pisa, south of Pisa, near the beach: Camping Internationale

Tourist office   At Camposanto and at the train station.

Marche

This popular tourist area on the Adriatic Ocean is overcrowded in July and August. Camping places are generally open May through September.

Camping places • Up and down the whole coast there are plenty of camping places.

Food market In Pesaro, behind the post office off P. del Popolo at via Branca 5, every morning

Gran Sasso

Named after the Appenine's highest peak, Gran Sasso is an excellent hiking area. Cable cars provide access to spectacular views and hiking trails.

Camping place • Northeast of L'Aquila, on A24, in Font Cerreto, just downhill from the funivia: Camping Funivia Del Gran Sasso

Tourist office	In l'Aquila, at P.Santa Maria. Take Corso Vittorio Emmanuele to via Leosino, then to P.Santa Maria Paganica 5.
Food market	At P.del Duoma, Monday through Saturday

NATIONAL PARK OF ABRUZZO

This is a wildlife preserve.

Camping places

• Several near Pescasseroli
• By the river on the Opi Road: Campeggio Dell' Orso

POMPEII, HERCULANEUM, AND MOUNT VESUVIUS

The fascinating remains of ancient volcanic eruptions that occurred here can be explored.

Camping places

• Near the ruins, outside of Villa dei Misteri: Camping Zeus and Camping Pompeii

Amalfi Coast

This strikingly beautiful rugged coastline is lined with high bluffs.

Camping place

• Close to Priano on the road to Amalfi: Camping place/Hotel La Tranquillita, via Roma 10; wonderful panoramic view of the coast

Northern Italy

GENOA

This city overflows with parks, fine palaces, and art museums.

Camping place

• West of Genoa, in Pegli: Camping Villa Doria, via Vespucci 25

RIVIERA DI PONENTE

This is a popular beach area around Genoa.

Camping places

- Near Calvisio, in Finale Ligure, via Piedmonte: Camping Del Mulino
- In Ventimiglia, close to the waterfront: Camping Roma via Peglia

Food market

In Ventimiglia via della Republica, every morning

Valle D'Aosta

This gorgeous mountain area is a haven for hikers, skiers, rafters, and kayakers.

Camping places

- In Les Fourches: Camping Ville D'Aosta
- In Roppoz: Camping Milleluci
- In Gignod: Camping Europa
- In Saint-Oyen: Camping Pineta, on the river
- In Brusson: Camping Deans

Tourist office

In Aosta, on P. Chanoux 8, down from Avenue du Conseil des Commis

GRAN PARADISO NATIONAL PARK

In this huge natural reserve, ibex and chamois now roam unharmed. There is a notable botanical garden in the Cogne Valley.

Camping places

- In Cogne: Camping Gran Paradiso
- Near Valnontey: Lo Stambecco

Tourist office

In Cogne, on P. Chanoux 34

MILAN

A cosmopolitan city that is a financial center for Italy, Milan epitomizes high style.

Don't miss:

- Duomo. It is architecturally memorable.
- La Scala. This is the world famous opera house and museum.
- Leonardo da Vinci's "Last Supper." You'll see it in the Cenacolo Vinciano, next to the Chiesa di Santa Maria delle Grazie.

Camping places
- Near S. Station and Aqua park: Camping Citta Milano, via Gaetano Airaghi 61
- In Barreggino: Il Bareggino, on via Corbettina
- In Monza: Autodromo, in the Park Villa Reale
- Southeast of Milan, off SS-9 towards Poaslo: Camping San Donato
- In Lana, off SS-238: Camping Schlosshof, Jaufen Str 10
- In Toblach, off SS-51: Camping Toblacher See.

Food market
In Milan around, Via Fauche; Saturdays

Dolomites and South Tyrol

This well-manicured area is a center for skiing and hiking.

Camping places
- In Dilmaro: Camping Dolomiti Di Brenta, on Passo d'el Tonale
- In Canazei, on SS-641 : Camping Mamolada, at the river

Venice and the Veneto

VENICE

Venice and its unique islands are jewels to be enjoyed and remembered forever.

Don't miss :

* San Marco Piazza. Absorb the atmosphere of the most famous square in the world.
* The Palazzo Ducale. This was once the seat of Venetian power and government.
* The Bridge of Sighs
* Galleria dell'Accademia. It houses important Venetian art.

But to really see Venice is to walk through its narrow winding streets, crossing some of its 400 bridges, and to ride the vaporetti through the canals.

Camping places

* At the beach, on the Adriatic side of the Lido (east of Venice), follow signs to Lido di Jesolo; many camping places. Prices vary considerably. Buses go to ferries that go to Venice and the other islands. It's magical to come into Venice by boat.

Food market

At the Rialto in Venice; great for taking photographs

VERONA

Built of rose-colored marble, Verona's magnificent Roman arena is the world-famous site of opera and ballet performances in July and August.

Camping places

* Just down from the castle: Campeggio Castel S. Pietro, on via Castel S. Pietro 54; within walking distance to the historic center
* North of the city, in Peschiera, on the road to Peschiera de Garda: Campeggio Romeo & Giulietta, via Bresciana 54

The Lakes Area

This region of beautiful crystal blue lakes is dotted with camping places.

LAGO DI GARDA
- In Cisano di Bardolion, off SS-249: Camping Casino
- In Lazise, off SS-249: Camping Quercia
- In Pievedi Manerba, off S572, close to Hotel Romantica: Camping Romantica
- In Moniga, off SS-572, by Ristorante La Pergola: Camping Delle Rosa
- In Sirmione, off S11: Camping Sirmione
- In Riva del Garda, off S456 or S240: Campeggio Bavaria, viale Rovereto 100

LAGO DI MAGGIORE
- Eastern shore, north end off SS-394, near Maccagno Inferiore: Maccagno Camping Ground
- In Angera, off S629, south of town: Camping Citta Di Angera
- In Fondotoce di Verbania, off SS-34, north of the Toce Bridge: Camping Isolino
- Close to Stresa, at Gignese: Sette Camini Residence

LAGO DI COMO
- In Sorico, off SS-340D: Camping Aulac Como; where the river enters the lake
- In Dongo, off SS 340D, at the traffic circle, toward the lake: Camping Alla Cigna Del Lago

Italian

Buon giorno

Hello

Per favore, dove _____?

Please, where is _____?

Puo scrivere, per favore.

Write it down, please.

Va sempre diritto _____ (meters/kilometers) a _____ (guardare Parolas Capisco).

Go straight ahead _____ (meters/kilometers) to the _____ (look at Words I Understand).

Il primo gira _____ (a destra/a sinistra) si va _____ (meters/ kilometers) a _____ (guardare Parolas Capisco).

First turn _____ (right/left) go _____ (meters/kilometers) to the _____ (look at Words I Understand).

Al prossimo gira _____ (a destra/a sinistra) si va _____ (meters/ kilometers) a _____ (guardare Parolas Capisco).

At the next turn _____ (right/left) go _____ (meters/kilometers) to the _____ (look at Words I Understand).

Quanto tempo a? _____ (minutos/oras)

How much time is it? _____ (minutes/hours)

Grazie

Thank you

List I Understand	Liste Paroles Capisco
corner	angolo
intersection	intersezione
stop sign	stop segno
traffic light	semafori
exit	usita
road/street	strade
highway	autostrada
large	grande
small	piccolo
far	lantano
near	vicino
bridge	ponte
river	fiume
woods	selva
lake	lago
sea	mare
harbor	rifugio
village/town	commune
city	citta
house	casa
train station	stazione F.S.
bus stop	fermata dell autobus
red	rosso
green	verde
blue	blu
yellow	giallo
white	bianco
black	nero
market place	mercato
supermarket	supermercato
gas station	stazione benzina
square	piazza
main square	piazza principale
castle	castello
cathedral	duomo
church	chiesa
camping place	campeggio
museum	museo
beach	spiaggia
ruins	rovine

Netherlands

Well-tended fields of flowers, windmills, and especially friendly people make The Netherlands popular with tourists. Because of its flat terrain, the country is ideal for biking.

Best time to go To see this flowering country in full bloom, visit in April and May, but be ready to share the joys of its beauty with plenty of other tourists. If you do go then plan to visit Keukenhof, where millions of flowers bloom in the world's largest garden. The sun shines most reliably May through August.

Shop hours Stores generally open at 9 A.M. and close at 6 P.M. Museums are closed on Mondays.

Tourist office Called the VVV; found in the tourist areas and also at the train stations

Camping places The Dutch love to camp. Their plentiful camping places are well run, friendly, and located in pleasant areas.

Driving It is easy to drive here because the roads are well marked. Traffic moves at a moderate rate and drivers are courteous to the bicyclist.

Food markets Check with the local VVV. Open markets are popular with the locals.

AMSTERDAM In this city filled with famous art museums, two of the most important are the Rijksmuseum, which honors Rembrandt, and the Van Gogh museum. The city has wonderful canalside cafes and is the starting point for interesting side trips to fishing villages, cheese farms, and wholesale flower and cheese markets.

Camping places
- Close to the city center: Zeeburg, Zuiker Ijdijk 44 and DE Badhoeve, at Uitdammerdijk 10
- Close to Schiphol airport, in Amsterdame Park: Camping Het Amsterdamse Bos

- On lake Gasper: Gaspercamping, at Loosdrechtdreef 7; close to public transportation to city center

Tourist office
- Leidsestrat 106
- Outside the central station (CS) at stationsplein 10

HAARLEM   A favorite of mine, this lovely little city is close to the beautiful Keukenhof Gardens. Biking is enjoyable in the pretty canalside neighborhoods and nearby farming areas.

Camping places
- At Liewegje 17: De Liede
- Near Zandvoort, in the sand dunes, several

Tourist office   Outside train station, at Stationsplein 1

LEIDEN

Europe's oldest botanical garden is located here.

Camping places

- Close by at Katwijk aan Zee, a beach area
- De Zuidduinen, at Zuidduinsewag 1
- De Noordduinen, at Campingweg 1

Tourist office

Stationsplein 210

THE HAGUE

The residence of the Dutch royalty, this refined city is near the miniature town of Madurodam.

Camping places

- On the coast in Scheveningen, Duinhorst, at Buurtweg 135
- Ockenburg, at Wijndaelrerweg 25

Tourist office

- Outside the central station (CS) at Koningin Julianaplein 30
- In Scheveningen, near the Kurhaus, at Geversdeynootweg 134

HOGE VELUWE

Hoge Veluwe is The Netherland's largest national park. The prestigious Kroller-Muller Museum, which houses 278 Van Goghs and many Picassos and Mondrians, is located within the park, and Europe's largest sculpture garden is next to the museum.

Camping places

- Close to the park; many
- Close to Arnhem: Arnhem Kampeer Centrum at Kemperberger-weg 771

German

Guten tag

Hello

Bitte, wo ist _____?

Please, where is _____?

Konnen sie es bitte aufschreiben.

Could you please write it down.

Gehen Sie geradeaus _____ (meters/kilometers) zu _____ (sehen Liste Ich Verstehe).

Go straight ahead _____ (meters/kilometers) to _____ (show me List I Understand).

Biegen Sie _____ (rechts/links) gehen _____ (meters/kilometers) zu _____ (sehen Liste Ich Verstehe).

Turn _____ (right/left) go _____ (meters/kilometers) to _____ (see List I Understand).

Nachste biegen _____ (rechts/links) gehen _____ (meters/ kilometers) zu _____ (sehen Liste Ich Verstehe).

Next turn _____ (right/left) go _____ (meters/kilometers) to _____ (see List I Understand).

Wie weit ist? _____ (minutes/stundes)

How long will it take? _____ (minutes/hours)

Danke

Thank you

List I Understand	Liste Ich Verstehe
corner	ecke
stop sign	stop zeichen
traffic light	stop signal
exit	ausgang
road/street	strade
highway	autostrada
large	gross
small	klein
far	weit
near	nahe
bridge	brucke
river	flub
woods	wald
lake	see
sea	mer
harbor	hafen
village	ort
town/city	stadt
house	haus
train station	bahnhof
bus stop	bushaltestelle
red	rot
green	grun
blue	blau
yellow	geld
white	weiss
black	schwarz
market place	marketplatz
supermarket	supermarket
gas station	benzin
square	platz
main square	haupplatz
castle	schloss
cathedral	Dom
church	kirche
camping place	campingplatz
old town	alstadt
museum	museum

Norway

The spectacular beauty of Norway's waterfall-laden fjords, rugged mountains, and blue glaciers draw tourists who love the out-doors. Adding to the enjoyment are the unspoiled fishing villages, preserved medieval towns, excellent museums, and scenic highways.

Some the most popular attractions are:

- Oslo's outstanding museums: Viking Ship Museum, Kon-Tiki Museum, Fram Polar Exploration Museum, and the Norwegian Folk Museum.

- The exceptionally well preserved and fortified seventeenth-century town of Fredrikstad, just outside of Oslo.

- The exciting train ride from Myrdal to Flam, one of the steepest tracks in the world.

- Ferry rides on Naeroyfjord and Geirangerfjord, the narrowest of Norway's fiords, both laden with waterfalls and picturesque-villages.

- The Jostedalspreen Glacier and Museum. Guided walks on the glacier are possible.

Best time to go   Norway has a short season for campers. June to mid-August are best. In the last two weeks of July many Norwegians are on vaca-tion. June and July are the months of the midnight sun, when there is very little darkness.

Camping places   They are expensive compared to southern Europe. Many have cabins, which are nice at rainy times. "Free" camping is permitted for tent campers because of the "everyman's right" law. This per-mits you camp in the wilderness for no longer than two nights at the same place and at least 150 meters from a dwelling. No fires are permitted, and you must not leave a trace of your stay. Asking for permission, if you are on farmland, is good etiquette.

Good equipment is essential for tent camping. The nights can be cold. Bring a warm jacket, long underwear, gloves, and a hat.

Driving

Traffic is very light and the scenery is beautiful. Mountain passes will be difficult for large camper vans. There are many hairpin turns. A few mountain passes are very narrow, requiring a driver to back up from approaching traffic. There are some long tunnels.

On the west coast, car ferries are part of the route. Pick up a time table from the local tourist office or ferry landing. Reservations usually aren't taken.

Driving laws are strictly enforced, and on-spot fines are issued. Headlights are required at all times when driving. Drinking and driving rules are strict and on-spot fines are very expensive. Observe speed limits carefully and wear seat belts. Have insurance documents and the red warning triangle inside the passenger area.

Tourist offices

They are located near the train station, dock, or town center. English is commonly spoken. Get a ferry time schedule. Buy a city tourist card if you plan to stay more than one day in a city. It includes admission to museums and attractions, local ferry rides, and parking. Information is available on camping places, river rafting, and summer skiing and fishing. Bookstores sell "Mountain Hiking in Norway" and "Motoring in Norway" by Welle-Strand.

Open markets

Fresh vegetables and fruit are sold along with fish at the harbor fish markets. Food is very expensive. Bring canned goods, pasta, coffee, tea, and the allotment of duty-free liquor into the country. Supermarkets have less expensive bread, fish, and meat than the specialty stores. Strong liquor, beer, and wine are sold only at *vin-monopols* (state stores). These stores often close at 4 P.M. during the week and at 1 P.M. on Saturday and are closed on Sundays. Shop early on a weekday.

Eating out

Dining out is expensive. For a treat enjoy the food at streetside kiosks, bakeries, and burger kebab and pizza places. Restaurant and cafeteria dining is less expensive for lunch when they offer *dagens rett*, or the daily special. The gratuity is included and no more is expected.

Shop hours

Usual hours during the week are 9 A.M. to 4 P.M. Some stores stay open until 6 P.M. on Thursdays and until 2 P.M. on Saturdays. On Sundays most stores are closed. Museums have short hours; they often open at 11 A.M. and close at 3 P.M.

OSLO

In this dignified city of parks and gardens, the highlights for travelers are the outstanding museums.

See:

- Viking Ship Museum. Ninth-century ships, well preserved in mud, were excavated and intricately restored and now display their burial holdings of furniture, jewelry, tools, and decorative items.
- Kon-Tiki Museum. See the balsa raft Kon Tiki, which Heyerdahl used to cross the Pacific from Peru to Polynesian, and the papyrus reed raft, Ra II, which he used to cross the Atlantic.
- Fram Museum. The polar ship Fram, launched in 1893, can be explored by visitors. The living quarters of men and dogs and photos of the exploration are fascinating.
- Norwegian Folk Museum. Norway's largest open-air museum, with its reconstructed farm buildings, stave church, homes, and workshops displaying tools, furniture, and china, bring to life seventeenth- and eighteenth-century living. Special events are held on the weekends.
- Akershus Castle. The underground dungeons, passages, and adjoining resistance museum are the highlights here.
- Vigeland Sculptural Park. Two hundred sculptural works of the artist can be viewed in this relaxing park, which is free and always open.
- Munch Museum. It houses 5,000 works by Norway's most famous artist.
- Holmenkollen Ski Jump Museum and Tryvannstarnet Tower. There are thrilling views and a fascinating display.
- Fredrikstak. This seventeenth-century, well-preserved, fortified town is not far from Oslo on the east side of the Oslofjord.
- Art Center at Hovikodden. This outstanding collection of modern art is not far from Oslo on the west side of the Oslofjord.

Tourist office

- West of the city center, close to the harbor at the old Oslo Vestbane station: Vestbaneplasses 1. Buying an Oslo Card will make museums, ferry and bus rides, and parking less expensive.
- Mollergata 3: Use It (has alternative information for youth and budget travelers)

The central railway station is called Oslo S and is on the east side of the city where Karl Johans Gate leads into the city center. Sights are either close by or easily reached by bus or ferry.

Camping places
- On a knoll above the city: Ekberg Camping, Ekeberhgveien 65
- Close to the lake in Holmenkollen: Bogstad Camping, Ankerveien 117
- On the Oslofjord island of Langoyene
- Free camping on the edge of Nordmarka, a wilderness area on Oslo's northern border, or away from the lake at Sognsvann

Open market
- Fruit and vegetable stalls in Jernbanetorget and at Basarhallene at the Karl Johans Gate
- At Torggata and Aker Brygge: Supermarket Rema 1000, has reasonable prices
- At the harbor, opposite Aker Brygge, well-priced freshly boiled fish

Parking
Pick up "How to Park in Oslo" at a gas station or camping place before entering the city. If you follow the signs for "Ring 1" you'll end at the Ibsen P-Hus underground parking area, which is close to Karl Johans Gate. There are other parking areas in the center of the city.

LILLEHAMMER   Site of the 1994 Winter Olympics, the area is now a popular sports area for families in winter and summer. North Europe's largest open air museum is here.

You can enjoy:

- Guided tours of the Olympic sites.
- Simulator rides of downhill skiing and bobsleighing.
- Exhibits at the Olympic Experience Center.
- Maihaugen Folk Museum. There are 140 buildings, including a stave church, farm buildings with farm animals, workshop demonstrations and participation, and people in period costumes. A free guided tour in English is available.
- Historic Vehicle Museum.
- World's oldest paddle steamer ride from Hamar to Lillehammer.
- Sjusjoon sports center for windsurfing, biking, horseback riding, and rowboats.

Camping places   • South of town on E6: Stranda Camping
- Others in the area

BERGEN

An important trading port in the middle ages, this city is dominated by the sea. A picturesque harbor, a university, and interesting museums make it worth exploring. Be ready for the rain that keeps it green and filled with flowers.

Special are:

- Torget. This is a hundred-year-old fish market.
- Bryggen Museum. The archeological museum, sitting on an eight-hundred-year-old foundation, houses excavated remains of medieval life, which are interestingly displayed.
- Hanseatic Museum. The sixteenth-century building has artifacts from the austere life of the Hanseatic merchants.
- Aquarium. There are large indoor and outdoor tanks and an adjoining pleasant park with an outdoor heated swimming pool.
- Mariakirken. The medieval church has fifthteenth-century frescos and a baroque pulpit.
- Edvard Grieg's home. Of interest to music lovers, Grieg's home is displayed just as he left it. In Hopsbroen follow signs to Troldhaugen.
- Ole Bull's Villa. This ornate villa, built by the famous violinist, is on the island of Lysoon. Take route 546 to Buena Kai, then take the car ferry.

Tourist office

On the main pedestrian street in Bryggen, on Torgalmenning

Camping places

- In Landas: Bergenshallens Camping, Vilh. Bjerknesvei 24; closest to city and often crowded
- East of the city on route 580, several

Open market

- Torget fish market at the harbor also has fruit and vegetable stalls.
- Mekka grocery chain has the best prices. There is one by the bus station where there are also fruit stalls, inexpensive sandwiches, and Chinese food.

AURLANDSFJORD AND FLAM

Taking the train ride from Myrdal to Flam, the steepest track in the world, is exciting. Tourists then board a ferry to enjoy the magnificent scenery of the Aurlandsfjord.

Camp at the lakeside camping places in Voss. Take the tiny train from Voss to Flam. The thrilling ride stops at a huge waterfall and goes through hand-dug tunnels. Have a picnic lunch at the picturesque tiny village of Flam, then board the ferry for a spectacular two-hour ride to Gudvangen. Connecting buses go up the beautiful valley back to Voss.

Camping place

• By the lake, past the church: Voss Camping.

JOSTEDALSPREEN GLACIER

The largest glacier on mainland Europe, this eight-hundred-square-kilometer ice plateau is a fascinating sight. An informative glacier center is located in Fjaerland. There are guided walks out on the glacier.

Camp in Balestrand. Take the ferry from Balestrand up the Fjaerlandsfjord to Fjaerland. Visit the Norsk Bremuseum, Glacier Center, which is on route 625 north of town. Guided glacier walking information is available here. Bring warm clothing if you plan to take a guided walk on the glacier.

Camping place

• In Balestrand, south along the fjord, past the English church, in an apple orchard: Sjotun Camping

Geirangerfjord

The waterfalls tumbling from the sheer walls of the Geirangerfjord are breathtaking. The trip can start at the car ferry at Hellesylt. A multilingual commentary describes the history of the area. Approaching the tiny village of Geiranger is unforgettably beautiful. After docking, follow a wonderful walking trail that leads to Storseter Waterfall. It passes between the rock face and the waterfall.

Camping place

• At the foot of the fjord: Geiranger Camping
• Others further away along the fjord

Tourist office

At the pier next to the post office

Romsdalsfjord and Trollveggen

This is a popular area for advanced mountain climbers. It can be reached by taking the Trollstigen Highway, a very narrow road with hairpin turns and breathtaking scenery. Route 9 between Dombas and Andalsnes is also beautiful. The Norsk Tinde Museum has expedition exhibits of the well-known mountaineer Heen.

Camping place
- In Andalsnes, several east of town

STAVANGER
This is the closest port for those arriving from England. The oil capital of Norway, it has an interesting historic harbor and well-preserved old town.

Sights to see include:
- Gamle Stavanger. This is a well-preserved old town with picturesque houses and gardens.
- Stavanger Domkirke. This notable twelfth-century church has organ recitals on Thursdays mornings.
- Canning factory. The reconstructed nineteenth-century sardine factory offers smoked sardine samples.

Tourist office
A short walk from Torget on the east side of Kulturhus, or town center

Camping places
- Beside the lake: Mosvangen Camping, next to the youth hostel
- Near the airport: Olberg Camping and Sola Camping

Open market
At the harbor on Torget: fruit, vegetable, and fish stalls

KRISTANSAND
The closest port to Denmark, this is a popular beach town for Norwegians.

Camping places
- East of town, across the river on the beach: Roligheden Camping, Marviksveien 100
- Free camping on off-shore islands or skerries

Norwegian

Goddag

Hello

Ver sa snill, kor er _____?

Please, where is _____?

Ver sa snill, a skrive.

Please, could you write it down.

Det er rett fram _____ (meters/kilometers) til _____ (se List Jeg Forstar).

Go straight ahead _____ (meters/kilometers) to _____ (see List I Understand).

Forste ta _____ (hogre/venstre) _____ (meters/kilometers) til _____ (se List Jeg Forstar).

First turn _____ (right/left) go _____ (meters/kilometers) to _____ (see List I Understand).

Neste ta _____ (hogre/venstre) skal _____ (meters/kilometers) til _____ (se List Jeg Forstar).

Next turn _____ (right/left) go _____ (meters/kilometers) to _____ (see List I Understand).

Kor mykje kommer er det? _____ (minuts/kommers)

How long will it take? _____ (minutes/hours)

Takk

Thank you

List I Understand	Liste Jeg Forstar
corner	hjornet
stop sign	stop stanna
traffic light	lyskrysset
exit	utgang
street/road	gate/vei
highway	motorveg
large	stor
small	litem
far	langt
near	naer
bridge	bro
river	elv
woods	skog
lake	innsjo
sea	sjo
harbor	havn
train station	jernbanestasjon
bus stop	busstop
red	raud
green	gron
blue	bla
yellow	gul
white	kvit
black	svart
market place	marknad-torget
supermarket	snarkjop
gas station	bensinstasjonen
main square	torget
castle	slott
cathedral	katedral/Domkirke
church	kirka
camping place	kamping
old town	gammelby
museum	museet
beach	strand
ruins	ruinar
waterfall	foss

Poland

Poland is the largest country in Europe. Its gently rolling hills, mountains, lakes, and coastline make it a grand place in which to enjoy the outdoors. Fine art collections, medieval castles and palaces, and lovely old towns add glamour to this wonderful country. The general flatness of the terrain, as well as roads that aren't heavily trafficked, make it a great cycling country.

Camping places

There are lots of camping places, both in the cities and in the countryside.

Driving

It is a well-marked country, not heavily trafficked and easy to drive in. It's harder to find unleaded gas, so if you are driving a vehicle that uses it, pick up (at the border) a list of stations that have unleaded. Diesel is easy to find. For regular gas, use 94 octane yellow or 98 octane red.

Tourist offices

Generally labeled IT or PTTK, offices are mostly open weekdays 9 A.M. to 4 P.M. and Saturday mornings. Be sure to bring good maps and a guide book from the United States.

Open markets

Open markets are here and there. Supermarkets are found near large housing units. Markets are better stocked in larger towns. Get bread, meat, and fish in the mornings. The markets aren't as well stocked as in western Europe, but prices are very reasonable and the quality is good.

WARSAW

The painstaking care given to rebuilding Warsaw after World War II is a tribute to the tenacity and pride of the people.

Be sure to see:

- Beautiful Pac Zamkowy Street. It leads into the old town, where Royal Way leads to the Royal Palace. Restoration is amazingly intricate.
- Lazienki Park and Palace. At the other end of Royal Way, the palace sits in the middle of a small lake. There, afternoon concerts are presented in memory of Chopin.

- Wilanow Palace. The interior of this baroque palace is as magnificent as the setting and grounds.
- National Museum. Included in the world-class collections of paintings is the magnificent painting of the Battle of Grumwald by Matejko.
- Chopin Museum. The museum is nearby at Zelazowa Wola.

Tourist office In old town, in a souvenir shop on Pac Zamkowy 1

Camping places
- Southeast of town on the road to the airport, ulica Zwirki i Wigury: Camping OST Gromada

ZAKOPANE This beautiful resort town, located south of Krakow in the Tatra Mountains, caters to skiers in the winter and hikers in the summer. To explore:
- Take the cable car at Kuznice to the summit of Kasprowy Wierch. Hikers can then walk down through the Gasienicowa Valley.
- Drive or take a bus to Polona Palenica. Then hike or rent a horse cart to go to the lake 9 km away. An easy, lovely trail around the lake can be hiked, or for the more energetic, follow the trail up to Mt. Rysy.

- See the architecturally interesting farming village of Chocholow.

Tourist office
- On the way from the railway station into town, ulica Kosciuszki 7
- Tatra National Park Information Office

Camping place
- Between town and Kugnice (the site of the cable car), on ulica Zeromskiego: Pod Krokiwiq. Follow the signs from the main road.

KRAKOW
- The largest medieval square in Europe is in Krakow's historic area. The Renaissance Cloth Hall, prominent in the square, is now a huge fine crafts market. Also be sure to see:
- Wawel Castle and Cathedral and Sigismund Chapel. This is considered to be the finest Renaissance construction in Poland.
- Czartoryski Art Museum. It has some very important individual pieces of art.
- Musical performances. The Filharmonia booking office is at ulica Zwierzyniecka 1.
- The salt mines at Wieliczka. These are a change of scene. There are other salt mines in Eastern Europe, but this one is one of the oldest and also has the largest underground chamber (St. Kinga Chapel). There are also intricately carved figures and an underground health clinic.
- The remains of the extermination concentration camps of Auschwitz and Birkenau. Auschwitz has green lawns and an important museum, while Birkenau has been left as it was.
- Pieskowa Skala. This is the most notable castle on the Eagle's Nest route from Krakow to Czestochowa.

Tourist office   Close to the railway station, ulica Pawia 8

Camping places
- Northwest corner of Krakow, at the junction of the highway from Katowice and Czestochowa: Camping Krakow
- South edge of Krakow, on the road to Zakopane, in a park with a public swimming pool

CZESTOCHOWA   This is the home of the Luminous Mountain Monastery, Jasna Gora, which houses the image of the Back Madonna—Poland's holiest icon. It is considered the most sacred place in Poland, and at dawn hundreds of nuns can be observed in silent prayer.

Camping place
- Near the monastery, on the other side of the tour bus parking lot: Camping Olenka

ZAMOSC   Originally designed by an Italian, this beautifully preserved Renaissance town has many parks and long, arched Italian-style homes in pastel shades.

Tourist office   Behind the Hotel Renesans, ulica Lukasinskiego 5A

Camping places
- West of town, close to the stadium: PTTK Camping, ulica Krolowej Jadwigi

Pomerania

Located on the Baltic coast, Pomerania has immense sand dunes, forests, and lagoons and is a popular vacation area with Poles.

LEBA   This small town has clean beaches and dramatic dunes. It is divided in half by Lebsko Lake. The beach on the west side of the lake is away from the town and is one of the best on the Baltic. Also, the largest shifting dunes in Eastern Europe are located here at Slowinski National Park. One of the dunes is forty-two meters high. The view from the top is excellent.

Camping places
- Just west of the railway station: Intercamp
- West of Intercamp and closer to the beach: Camping Przmorz

SOPOT   This is Poland's most fashionable seaside resort. Lively music festivals are held in the forest behind town in summer.

Tourist office   PTTK Bohaterow Monte Cassino 31

Camping places
- Near the beach between Gdansk and Sopot: Jelitkowo Camping place

- Closer to the beach, north of Jelitkowo on the main road: Sopot Camping

GDANSK

Poland's largest port, Gdansk, the birthplace of the Solidarity Movement, was home to astronomer Hevelius, physicist Fahrenheit, and philosopher Schopenhauer. Medieval Gdansk was one of the richest ports in Europe. Excursion boats on the Baltic provide an interesting way for tourists to capture the feeling of this famous old town. For a longer boat ride go across the Baltic from Gdansk to the small fishing village of Hel.

Tourist office

Across from the railroad station on ulica Heweliusza 8

Camping places

- Near the wharf: Camping Brzena, ulica Karola Marlsa 234
- East of Gdansk, on the coast road towards Stegna, at the beach, by the pine forest.

Polish

Dzieh Dobry

Hello

Prosze, gdzie jest _____?

Please, where is _____?

Prosze, czy mogl bys to zapisac.

Please, could you write it down.

Prosto _____ (meters/kilometers) do _____ (prosze mi Liste Rozumiem).

Go straight ahead _____ (meters/kilometers) to _____ (show me List I Understand).

Prawol/lewo _____ (meters/kilometers) do _____ (prosze mi Liste Rozumiem).

Go right/left _____ (meters/kilometers) to _____ (show me List I Understand).

Nastepny prawol/lewo _____ (meters/kilometers) do _____ (prosze mi Listye Rozumiem).

Next go right/left _____ (meters/kilometers) to _____ (show me List I Understand).

Jak dhugo trwa podroz? _____ (minuty/ktorej)

How long will it take? _____ (minutes/hours)

Dziekuje

Thank you

List I Understand	Liste Rozumiem
next corner	najblizszym rogu
stop sign	stop
traffic light	stop lampa
exit	wyjscie
road	droga
street	ulica
highway	autostrada
large	wieki
small	mahy
far	deleko
near	blisko
bridge	most
river	rzeka
woods	las
lake	jezioro
harbor	port
village	wies
town/city	miasto
train station	stacja kolejowa
bus stop	prystanek autobusowy
red	czerwony
green	zielony
blue	niebieski
yellow	zolty
white	bialy
black	czarny
market place	targ/bazar
supermarket	sam spozywczy
gas station	stacja benzynowa
square	plac
main square	glowny plac
old town square	rynek
castle	zamek
cathedral	katedra
church	kosciot
camping place	camping
old town	stare miasto
palace	palac
cave	jaskinia
waterfall	wodospad

Portugal

Portugal is a friendly, unpretentious country with scenic coast-lines, fishing villages, and bustling street markets. The seafood is delicious, the bullfights are like ballets, and the soccer games are exciting. Many fiestas and processions provide opportunities to experience traditional music and dress. Museums are closed on Monday.

Best time to go   Because of its proximity to the ocean, Portugal has a temperate climate. In the Algarve and Alentejo regions, the tourist season is from late February through November. In northern Portugal, it is May through September.

Shop hours   Typically stores open at 10 A.M. and close at 5 P.M., also closing for a lunch break.

Tourist offices   Known as postos de turismo or tourismos, they are usually located on the main square.

Camping places   Plentiful throughout the country. On the south coast, they are usually open all year and are very inexpensive. More elaborate, expensive camping places are available. In areas where there isn't a camping place, it is often possible to make arrangements with a farmer to camp on his land for the night. *Roterio Campista,* a multilingual guide to camping places throughout Portugal, can be found in most bookstores.

Driving   Driving isn't difficult, but Portuguese roads are not up to northern European standards and drivers drive fast. Several modern toll roads connect the major cities, but the smaller country roads are more scenic.

Open markets   Called mercado or fiestas, the street markets are plentiful. Visit them to buy fresh seafood, vegetables, and fruit as well as to absorb the local atmosphere.

LISBON

This hilly, unpretentious city on the River Tagus is the capital of Portugal and the site of most of the country's major museums, bullfights, and soccer games.

Sightseeing

Be sure to see:

In the Alfama District:

- Castelo de Sao Jorge. To get there, take Tram #28, which winds through the narrow streets and then up the steep hill.
- Museu de Arts Decorativa.

In the Belem District:

- Jeronimos Monastery. Manueline architecture is at its height here.
- Torre de Belem. This is a popular photo spot.
- Museu dos Coches (royal coaches museum.)
- Museu de Marinha (maritime museum.)

In the Xabregas District:

- Gulbenkian Museum. It houses a wide variety of both ancient and modern fine arts from western and eastern Europe.
- Museu dos Azulejos, inside the church of Madres de Deus. The beautiful tiles for which Portugal is renowned are here.

In the Bairro Alto:

- Hear Fado. This is music whose roots were originally African but which has been influenced over many years by maritime, colonial, and protest movements. It is reminiscent of the French chansons. There is also good African and Brazilian music.

Camping places

- In Monsanto Park, northwest of the city: Parque De Turismo E Campismo De Monsanto; many semi-permanent campers
- At Oeiras, on N-6 towards Estoril, near the train station and municipal garden: Paque De Campismo Muncipal
- At the beach on the Costa da Caparica, about an hour from Lisbon, nicer campsites but also costlier

Tourist office

At Praca dos Restauradores, Palacio Foz, has current information about the soccer games and bullfights

Open market	Mercado da Ribeira, opposite the Cais do Sodre train station in the Baixa area, an especially good morning market

Just North of Lisbon

SINTRA

Sightseeing	This small picturesque town is set on a hillside close to the coast.

See the:

- Palacio Nacional de Sintra (Royal palace). Informal guided tours are available.
- Palacio de Pena. This is a good example of expansive architecture and decoration.
- Monserrate Gardens in Colares
- Cork Convent. These tiny dwellings are carved from the rock and lined in cork by the resident monks.

Camping places	- Just outside of Sintra on the N-247 from Colares: Camping Capuchos - On the beach in Praia Grande: Camping Praia Grande
Tourist office	In the museum on the Praca da Republica
Food market	In Sao Pedro both a flea market and a food market are held on the second and last Sundays of the month.

Just West of Lisbon

ESTORIL AND CASCAIS	These beach resort areas are favored by tourists.
Camping place	- Just north of Cascais, on the way to Sintra, at Guincho Beach: Orbitur Do Guincho

Southern Coast of Portugal/ The Algarve

The sunny beaches here are very popular with European tourists.

FARO

The capital of The Algarve, this is a good place to pick up information on the rest of this area.

Tourist office

In Faro, on Rua da Misericordia

TAVIRA

This is one of the oldest and loveliest of the towns in The Algarve.

Camping places

• Camping places are plentiful.

Food market

In Largos, at the intersection of Rua dos Portas and Avenida dos Descobrimentos, on Monday and Saturday mornings

Central Portugal

EVORA

A well-preserved, walled town, Evora is architecturally one of Portugal's gems. It is scenically set among olive groves, vineyards, and wheat fields.

Located close together are:

- Temple of Diana.
- Museu de Evora.
- Evora Cathedral.

Get the walking tour map at the tourist office.

MONSARAZ   This charming walled village is set high up on a mountain and has views of the fertile plains below.

VILA VICOSA   The private apartments of Dom Carlos at Paco Ducal are home-like. There are large collections of furniture and art at the palace as well as lovely gardens.

Camping place   • Just south of Evora, in the direction of Alcacovas: Orbitur

Tourist office   On the main square in Evora, Praca do Giraldo 73

Food market   In Evora, in the parking lot just outside the southern wall of the town, close to the church of Sao Bras, Tuesday and Saturday mornings

North Along the Atlantic Coast

BERLENGA ISLAND   In nice weather this can be an all-day adventure. Start early, bring a picnic lunch, and take the one-hour ferry ride to Peniche. Once there, explore the island's jagged coastline of caves and fiords. If the sea is calm, you can snorkel, rent a row boat, or take a tour boat through the Furado Grande, a 75-meters-long tunnel with a beautiful cove at the end. Camping is limited.

NAZARE   Set on a beautiful coastline, this picturesque fishing village is well known for its seafood.

ALCOBACA   The monastery, church, kitchen, and cloisters of the impressive Santa Maria Monastery here are worth a detour.

OBIDOS   It is possible to walk along the top of the ancient ramparts in this
                     well-preserved, medieval walled town.

Camping places   • Close to Nazare, at Pederneira: Camping Golfino
                     • East side of Nazare, off the highway 8-4, in the pines: Orbitur
                       Camping Valado
                     • In the same area, closer to the beach: Camping Pedralva

Northern Portugal

OPORTO   The second largest city in Portugal, Oporto is set on the river
                     Douro. Its famous wines can be sampled in the port wine lodges
                     on the south side of the river in Vila Nova de Gaia. From Oporto,
                     drive through the spectacular scenery of the Valley of the River
                     Douro. You'll enter a gorge, pass through lovely traditional villages
                     (Amarante is particularly enjoyable), and see the famous vine-
                     yards planted on the steep sides of the area's mountains.

Camping places   • In the northwest suburb of Oporto: Parque De Campismo Da
                       Prelada; bus to city center
                     • In Madalena, south of Oporto: Camping Marisol

Tourist office   Close to the town hall, at Rua Clube dos Fenianos

Open markets   • Just off Avenida dos Aliados

North of Oporto on the Coast

VIANA DO   Singing and dancing festivals are held here in August. Renais-
CASTELO   sance Square, the Praca de Republica, is considered to be Portu-
                     gal's most beautiful square. Locals create traditional handicrafts,
                     so it is a good place to buy them.

Camping places   • North of Viana do Castelo, on the beach in Ancora

Open market   In Barcelos, at the the Campo da Republica, on Thursdays, very
                     large

Close to the Northern Spanish Border

PENEDA-GERES NATIONAL PARK   The largest natural preserve in Portugal, the Peneda-Geres encompasses wooded hills, streams, reservoirs, and gorges.

Camping place

- In Vidoeiro, on the edge of town alongside a river, operated by the park

Tourist office   In Caldas dos Geres, provides information on hiking, flora, and fauna

Portuguese

Bom dia

Hello

Por favore, para ir a _____?

Please, where is _____?

Podo escreve-lo, por favor.

Could you write it down, please.

Siga sempre a direito _____ (meters/kilometers) para _____ (ver Liste Entendo).

Go straight ahead _____ (meters/kilometers) to _____ (see List I Understand).

Primeira vire _____ (direita/esquerda) _____ (meters/kilometers) para _____ (ver Liste Entendo).

First turn _____ (right/left) go _____ (meters/kilometers) to _____ (see List I Understand).

Proximo vire _____ (direita/esquerda) siga sempre _____ (meters/ kilometers) para _____ (ver Liste Entendo).

Next turn _____ (right/left) go _____ (meters/kilometers) to _____ (see List I Understand).

Quanto temp dura? _____ (minutos/horas)

How long will it take? _____ (minutes/hours)

Obrigado

Thank you

List I Understand	Liste Entendo
corner	esquina
intersection	interseccion
stop sign	stop
traffic light	senalado
exit	salada
road	estrada
street	rua
highway	autostrada
large	grande
small	piqueno
far	longe
near	perto
bridge	ponte
river	rio
woods	bosque
lake	lago
sea	mar
harbor	puerto
town	localidad
city	cidade
house	casa
train station	estacao de comboios
bus stop	paragem de autocarro
red	vermelho
green	verde
blue	azul
yellow	amarelo
white	branco
black	preto
market place	mercado
grocery store	supermercado
gas station	estacao gasolinera
square	praca
main square	praca principal
castle	castelo
cathedral	catedral
church	igreja
camping place	parque de campismo
old town	cidade velha
beach	praia
museum	museu

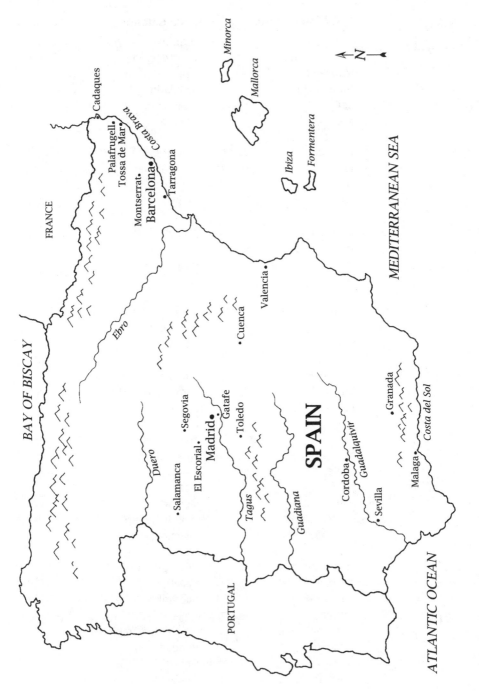

Spain

Spain is a longtime favorite for Europeans because of its long stretches of beaches and sunny weather. Spain is also known for its exciting cultural life, museums, and historic squares.

Besides enjoying the beaches, try to see some of these:

- Prado Museum in Madrid. It houses one of the finest art collections in the world.
- Archaeological Museum in Eruel, Aragon. It is one of the best of its kind.
- Museo de Bellas Arts in Bilbao. This is listed with Europe's best art museums.
- Exciting architecture and modern art in Barcleona.
- Medieval Aqueduct in Segovia.
- The Alhambra. A romantic palace in Granada.
- Toledo. Enjoy its dramatic setting.
- Immense mosque in Cordoba.
- Historic squares in Salamanca, Santiago de Compostela, and Mojacar.
- Prehistoric cave paintings in Altamira.

Best time to go

By mid-April it is predictably warm in the south. The beaches will be pleasant in mid-October. Summer months will be hot and crowded.

Camping places

Camping is popular and camping places are plentiful, particularly close to the beaches.

Driving

Spain's drivers are not as mindful of road rules, and they seem to park anywhere. But vehicles are towed from illegal parking areas, and retrieving your vehicle is expensive. Bring your proof of membership in your local auto club for reciprocal agreements with RACE (447-3200), a 24-hour emergency service.

Food markets

Every town has a mercado. Shop there for the best price on fresh food and to absorb the local atmosphere.

Tourist offices	In every large town and city, centrally located
Shop hours	Shops open at 9 A.M. and close for lunch at 2 P.M. If they reopen, it is generally from 5 P.M. to 8 P.M. Museums are closed on Mondays.
Eating out	Food in Spain is part of nightlife entertainment. Snacks are delicious. Use your guidebook for recommended places to enjoy many of the Spanish specialties. Less expensive is the plato combinado or combination plate. Some service charge is usually included, but leave the change and five to ten percent more if the service has been good.

MADRID

Once the capital of the world's largest empire, this tree-lined city has impressive boulevards, exciting nightlife, and exuberant futbol (soccer) games. Use the metro (underground rapid transit) to get around in the city.

Try to see:

- El Prado Museum. It is one of the greatest art museums in the world. (Use metro stop Banco de Espana or Atocha.) Start at the ground floor of the north end to see the art in chronological order. A guidebook helps in this immense museum.
- Cason del Buen Retiro. It houses Picasso's El Guernica as well as an excellent collection of other Spanish masterpieces. (Take the same metro stops as for the Prado. It is between the Prado and the Parque de Buen Retiro.) Tickets for the Prado cover this museum too.
- Archaeological Museum. It traces the past from the earliest cave paintings. (Use metro stop Colon or Serrano.)
- Panteon de Goya. Goya's ceiling and dome painting in the tiny church is considered some of his finest work. (Take metro Nor.)

Camping places

- North of the city: Camping Madrid
- Near the airport on the Ajalvir-Vicalvaro Road, Exit 12: Camping Osuna
- In Getafe: Camping Alpha

Tourist offices

- At Pl. Mayor (metro Sol), at the international arrival area at the airport
- In Torre de Espana on Plaza de Espana

It's helpful to pick up:

- Guia de Camping Espana—for more details on camping
- Madrid: Museums and Monuments—a detailed brochure
- Information on El Escorial

Metro (underground rapid transit)

The system is clean and well run. Get a metro map, *Plano del Metro*, at a metro ticket office and also *billete de diez*, a discounted ticket. The direction you want is the stop at the end of the line you will be traveling on.

EL ESCORIAL

This immense but severe monastery, museum, palace, basilica, and library is one hour from Madrid. It is closed on Monday.

Tourist office

- At C. Floridablanca 10
- Best information is in Madrid's tourist office.

Camping place

- Just outside of town: Caravaning El Escorial, Ctra. on de Guadarrama a El Escorial

Mercado

Just off C. Floridablanca on C. del Rey 9

SALAMANCA

This city is historically important because Spain's oldest university is here. The facades of the golden sandstone buildings here are elegantly faced.

While here enjoy:

- Plaza Mayor. It is one of Spain's most beautiful squares.
- Catedral Nueva. This is a huge, elegant structure.
- Universidad. The filigree work of silversmiths (Plateresque) in the entryway is exquisite.

Tourist office

At Pl. Mayor (Get Ambiente, for information on current happenings.)

Camping places

- Toward Madrid: Camping Regio
- Toward Aldealengua: Don Quijote

SEGOVIA

Inhabited for thousands of years, this proud city is on the UNESCO's World Heritage list.

Don't miss:

- Aqueducto Romano. This amazing Roman feat of 50 B.C. is magnificently preserved.
- Catedral. On the main square, the Gothic church is called the Queen of Cathedrals.
- Alcazar. This dramatic fortress has an interesting history, and the view of the Castille plains is excellent from the *torre*, or tower.
- The ancient, twisty alleyways of the old city.
- La Granja. Southwest of Segovia, it is considered Spain's Versailles and houses one of the world's best collections of Flemish tapestries.

Tourist office

- Next to the cathedral, Pl. Mayor, 10.
- At the aqueduct, Pl. Azoquejo

You'll need a map for this ancient city.

Camping place

- On the road to La Granja: Camping Acueducto

Mercado

Off C. Cronista Lecea on C. Colon

CUENCA

Tourists come to see the houses that are precariously hanging from the cliffs here. There is a notable abstract art museum. Children enjoy picnics at Ciudad Encantada or Enchanted City, where unusually shaped rocks are given names.

TOLEDO

This ancient city, built dramatically on a rock, possesses rich history. Steep, winding streets and collections of Spanish treasures have made it a very popular place with tourists.

Important attractions here are:

- Inglesia de San Tome. El Greco's masterpiece Burial of Conde de Orgazi, is on view here.
- Museo de la Santa Cruz. This is the home of other masterpieces of El Greco, including Le Asuncion.
- Alcazar. Historically important, it has an extensive collection in the military museum.

Tourist offices

- North side of town at the bottom of the hill, across from the Bisagra gateway to the old town
- Pl. Zocodover: an information booth

Get a map for the sights on top of the hill. The streets are like a labyrinth.

Camping places

- Road from Madrid, C-401, close to the Tajo River: Camping El Greco
- Close to the city: Cico Romano, Av. Carlos III 19; not as nice

Mercado

At Pl. Mayor behind the Cathedral

BARCELONA

This is one of the world's greatest cities. Its modern architecture, inspired by Gaudi, is internationally known. Important Picasso and Miro museums are here. Use the tourist bus, which passes most of the important points of interest. You can get on and off to spend time where you want.

While here enjoy:

- Sagrada Familia. These are Gaudi's eight masterful towers. After a climb to the top there is a view of the sea.
- Parc Guell. Gaudi's works and home are here. (Take metro to Vallarca, then walk to Bixada de la Gloria.)
- Picasso and Miro museums. (Take metro Jaume and Espanya.)
- Las Rambles. It is a beautiful boulevard.
- Barri Gotic and Barri de la Ribera. These are the old and the new Barcelona.
- Gran Theatre del Liceu. See this world-famous opera house.

Tourist office	At Gran Via 658
Mercado	Mercat de St. Josep, Rambla San Josep 89; modern steel building
Camping places	• Closest to the city: Camping Barcino, Carrer Laurea Miro 50; get there early
	• South of the city: Camping Cala Gogo, Carretera de la Platja
	• On the beach, south of the city in Gava: Albatros and Tortuga Ligera
	• On route N-246, south of the city, between km 11 and km 17, other camping places

MONTSERRAT   Dramatically set high up on a rocky peak, the monastery attracts pilgrims who come to see the Black Virgin Mary. There are wonderful views from various hiking paths. A boys chorus sings at 1 P.M.

Camping place   • Up the hill from the St. Joan funicular

TARRAGONIA   The town was settled by Romans in 218 B.C. An important archaeological museum here makes it worth a stop. Monestir Poblet, an immense and architecturally beautiful Cistercian abbey, is close by.

Tourist office   At Rambla Nova 46

Camping place   • On the beach, north of town along CN-340, several

Costa Brava

The coastal area from Barcelona north to France was named brava because of its craggy precipices and high winter winds. But in the late spring, summer, and early fall it attracts sunseekers who are looking for remote beach coves. Chagall and Dali worked here, and the largest collection of Dali's work is housed in Cadaques. There are snorkeling and boat trips to the coral reefs in the national park. Hiking and outdoor concerts are other attractions.

Tourist office

In Tossa de Mar at the bus terminal, Av. Pelegri 25

Camping places

- In Tossa de Mar, on the road to Lloret: Cala Lievado
- On the road to St. Feliu: Camping Caravaning Pola
- In Cadaques: Camping Cadaques, Ctra. Portilligat, 17
- Close to Palafrugell, in Tamariu: Camping Tamariu

Baleraric Islands Area

Tourists come here for the brilliant sunsets, turquoise sea, white sandy beaches, and exciting nightlife. Bicycling, hiking, moped riding, and boating are all popular pastimes.

Special are:

- Cape Formentor. This is a dramatic area. Walk from it to Soller to Deia.
- Minorca's old stone walls and picturesque whitewashed houses.
- The nightlife on Ibiza.

Tourist offices
- On Majora, in Palma, Avinguda Jaume III (If you like hiking, pick up "Rambler's Paradise" for hiking into the dramatic Serra de Tramuntana.)
- On Minorca, in Mahon, Plaza de la Conquista and Plaza de la Explanada (Get information on the archaeological sites.)
- On Ibiza, in Ibiza, Carrer Vara de Rey 13

Camping places
- On Majorca, near Alcudia, east of town near the Monastery Victoria, at the hostel, Ctra Pinar
- On Minorca, near Cala Galdana
- On Ibiza, near Santa Eulalia: Es Cana and Florida and west of Sant Antoni on the bay: Cala Bassa

Mercados
- On Majorca, in Palma, near C. Pl. Espanya off C. Padre Atanasio and in Alcudia in the center of town, Tuesday and Sunday mornings
- On Minorca, in Mao, off Pl. Carme
- On Ibiza, in San Penya near the old gate to D'alt Vila, on Pl. Constitucio

VALENCIA
Valencia is reputed to be the founding town of paella, a delicious combination of shellfish, chicken, sausage, and saffron rice. Visitors also find enjoyable:

- Palacio de Marques. This extravagant baroque structure also houses the Museo de Ceramica.
- Castell de Morella. The ruins of this ancient fortress are impressively set, high on a rocky crag. The old town is enclosed by a wall.

Tourist office	Plaza del Ayuntamiento
Camping place	• South of town in El Saler
Mercado	Plaza del Mercado

Andulusia

SEVILLA

This is an exciting city, particularly during the festivals of Semana Santa, a solemn but beautiful festival during Easter week, and Feria de Abril, a lively flamenco festival fifty days after Easter. Locals are proud of the Cathedral of Santa Maria de la Sede, the largest gothic structure in the world. After a climb up the Moorish tower Girald, there is a wonderful view of the city. The Archivo de las Indias is one of the most important archives in the world. Fascinating maps are on display.

Tourist office

Close to the cathedral, Avenida de la Constitution

Camping places

• Near the airport, Ctra. Madria-Cadiz highway km 534: Camping Sevilla

• Outside of town, Ctra. Sevilla-Dos Hermanas: Club de Campo, Av. Libertad 13; swimming pool

• Close to Italica, Ctra. Sevilla-Cadiz highway km 554: Camping Villsom

Mercado

Near the bull ring, Calle Arenal

GRANADA

The Islamic legacy in this city is the greatest in Europe. Its narrow winding streets are fascinating to explore, but most of all, people come to see the fabulous Alhambra, a tribute to Islamic art and architecture.

Tourist office

On the south side of Plaza Bib-Rambia, in Arco de Cucharas

Camping places

• Closest to town: Sierra Nevada, Av. Madrid, 107

• On the Malaga road, Ctra. National 342 highway km 292: Maria Eugenia and Los Alamos

• On the Zubia road, Ctra. Granada km 4: Reina Isabel; shuttle bus to historic Granada

Mercado	Beside the cathedral at Pl. Romanilla

CORDOBA Mezquita, the immense mosque built by the Moors and later enlarged by the Christians, is this city's important historic sight. In the Patio de los Naranjos, there are 850 columns supporting hundreds of two-tiered arches.

Tourist offices
- Near the entrance of the mosque on Calle Torrijos
- In the Jewish quarter, on the western side of the Mezquita, Pl. Judas Levi

Camping places
- North of the train station, off Av. America: Campamento Municipal, Av. Brillante
- Outside of town, on Ctra. Aldea de Quintana a Santaella km 11: La Campina; swimming pool

Mercado Plaza de la Corredera

Basque Country

SAN SABASTIAN Known as Donostia to the locals, this city is close to the Spanish and French border. It has a beautiful city beach, La Concha, and lively nightlife. International surfing competitions take place just west of the city in Zarautz.

Tourist offices
- In Teatro Victoria Eugenia, on C. Reina Regente
- On Avenida de la Republica Argentina and El Boulevar

Camping places
- At Zarautz, west of San Sabastian, on the beach
- At Mundaka, north of Guernica, Calle Potuondo 1

Mercado In Bermeo, close to Mundaka

Spanish

Buenos dias

Hello

Por favore, dode esta _____?

Please, where is _____?

Puede escribirlo, por favor.

Could you write it down, please.

Vaya todo _____ (meters/kilometers) para _____ (sede Lista Comprendo).

Go straight ahead _____ (meters/kilometers) to _____ (see List I Understand).

Primer doble _____ (derecha/izquierda) vaya _____ (meters/ kilometers) para _____ (sede Liste Comprendo).

First turn _____ (right/left) go _____ (meters/kilometers) to _____ (see List I Understand).

Prosimo _____ (derecha/izquierda) vaya _____ (meters/kilometers) para _____ (sede Liste Comprendo).

Next turn _____ (right/left) go _____ (meters/kilometers) to _____ (see List I Understand).

Cuanto dura el viaje? _____ (minuto/hora)

How long is the trip? _____ (minutes/hours)

Gracias

Thank you

List I Understand	Lista Comprendo
intersection	interseccion
stop sign	stop signo
traffic light	stop senalado
exit	salida
road/street	calle
highway	autostrada
large	grande
small	pequeno
far	legos
near	cerca
bridge	puenta
river	rio
woods	bosque
lake	lago
sea	mar
harbor	puerto
village/town	localidad
city	ciudad
house	casa
train station	estacion
bus stop	parada de autobus
red	rojo
green	verde
blue	azul
yellow	amarillo
white	blanco
black	negro
market place	mercado
grocery store	supermercato
gas station	estacion gasolinera
square	plaza
main square	plaza mayor
castle	castillo
cathedral	catedral
church	iglesia
camping place	terreno de camping
old town	ciudad antiqua
beach	playa

FINLAND

N

SWEDEN

GULF OF BOTHNIA

Mora

Lake Siljan Rattvik

Falun

Uppsala

Archipelago Stockholm

NORWAY

Visby

Mariestad Vadstena

Bohuslan Lake Vattern

Gothenburg

NORTH SEA

BALTIC SEA

Lund

Malmo

Sweden

Brilliant lakes, magnificent forests, abundant parks, and impressive cultural sights are Sweden's attractions.

People enjoy:

* Ferry trips on the Archipelago.
* Vasa Ship and Skansen Folk Museums in Stockholm.
* Bicycling. There are scenic cycling routes that are off the main highways. Rentals are available.
* Canoeing. Canoeing centers offer rentals, lessons. and guides for lake and river canoeing.
* Walking and hiking. Wonderful trails are plentiful. Some have mountain centers and huts that offer food and showers.

Best time to go By late May and through early September it is usually warm and sunny. July is crowded because the Swedes are vacationing. June and July are the months of the midnight sun, when there is very little darkness. August can be rainy but also warm. It is important to bring a raincoat, umbrella, and warm jacket, because the weather conditions change quickly.

Camping places Excellent camping places, many with kitchens, are plentiful. Camping places are open May through August. Bring an international camping carnet card or buy a national camping card at the first camping place. Free tent camping is allowed under common access right, *allemans ratten,* on uncultivated land that is away from dwellings and only for one night with a small tent. Pick up "Camping Sverige," a comprehensive listing of camping places, at large camping places or a smaller free list from the tourist office. Stock up on camping gas for your stove when you can; not all camping places have it.

Driving The roads are excellent, and the traffic is light. Headlights are required at all times when driving. Give right of way to pedestrians at crossings marked by zebra lines and to cyclists at cycle tracks marked by broken lines on either side. Slower vehicles are expected to move into paved edges so that faster traffic can pass. In large cities parking is paid for by tickets obtained at a P-Automat.

Small directional signs point to the location of the automat. (See Appendix: Parking.) In the north, reindeer and elk on the roads can be a hazard at dawn and dusk. If an accident occurs, it must be reported.

Tourist office   English is spoken and many brochures and maps are given out free. The large, detailed city maps are inexpensive. Buy a city tourist card if you plan to explore the city for more than a day. The card includes admission to museums and attractions, local ferry and bus rides, and parking.

Open markets   Farmers markets are not as common in Sweden as they are in other parts of Europe. Get the *Svensk Lantmat* list detailing local farms, dairies and smokehouses where you can buy on-site. Food is expensive. Bring canned goods, pasta, coffee, tea, and the allotted duty-free liquor into the country with you. Strong alcoholic beverages are sold only at a systembolaget, a state-controlled store that is open only on *weekdays* and closes at 5 P.M. Shop early in the day and bring identification. Wine is reasonably priced.

Eating out   Dining out is costly. Breakfast and lunch are less expensive than dinner. For lunch, reasonable choices will be husmanskost (often meatballs and potatoes), sallad (cold slaw and roll), and dageno ratt, (daily special, which will include bread, salad, and coffee). Ethnic restaurants and pizza places are good choices for evening meals. A service charge of 10 percent is included, but if the service has been good leave some extra.

STOCKHOLM   Surrounded by water, the city sits on a group of islands. Gamala Stan, the old city, is in the center. East is Djurgarden, a huge park containing Skansen, the Vasa ship museum, and gently rolling parkways.

You won't want to miss:

- Gamala Stan. See the ceremonial buildings with exquisite latticework and medieval walkways. Get a walking tour map from the tourist office.

- Skansen. This is old-fashioned Sweden. There are 150 reconstructed buildings, windmills, regional farms, craft-persons, folk dancing, and an excellent zoo. Take the mini train to the top of the hill and work your way down. The lack of commercialism is refreshing.

- Vasamuseet. This huge warship, Vasa, built in the 1600s, sank. It was preserved for three hundred years in mud. Now restored, it is impressively housed in a museum at the water's edge. There are excellent displays of daily life aboard.
- Drottningholm. Gracefully located on the lake, this royal palace is still home to royalty. A tour of the Court Theatre gives visitors the fun of seeing eighteenth-century special theater effects. Take the ferry; it's a one-hour trip from Stockholm.
- Mariefred. This is a tiny village with a grand castle, railway museum, narrow-gauge steam engine train, and good biking trails. Camping is available. The steamboat ride from Stockholm is 3 ½ hours.

Tourist office Ground floor of Sweden House, northwest corner of Kungstradgarden on Hamngatan. It can be a confusing city with its many water- and park-ways, so buy the detailed city map. Pick up a free camping place brochure and "Stockholm This Week." The Stockholm Card, bought here, will cover most of your sightseeing needs at a discount. Park on Regeringsgatan or take the metro to Kungstradgarden.

Camping places
- For camper-vans only, closest to the city, behind the Stockholm Stadium: Ostermalms Husvagncamping, Fiskartorpsvagen
- For camper-vans only, close to Eriksdalsbadet swimming pool: Sodermalms Husvagncamping
- Southwest of the city, near the beach in Bredang: Bredang Camping, Stora Sallskapets vag
- Southeast of the city in Slussen: Flatens Camping
- West of the city, near the beach, in Angbyplan: Angby Camping

Open market
- In Hotorget, off Sveavagen, an outdoor produce market, closed Sunday (Ethnic food stalls of Hotorgshallen are underneath.)
- At Ostermalms Torg, inside Ostermalmshallen, upscale food stalls of fish, cheese, and other delicacies, closed Sunday.

UPPSALA This is a quiet medieval university town where the largest cathedral in Scandinavia, Domkyrkan, is located. Linne Museum and garden at Svartbacksgatan 27 has memorabilia of the great scientist Carl von Linne.

Tourist office At Fyris torg 8

Camping places
- Free tent camping in open space of Gamla Uppsala
- At lake Malaren: Graneberg Camping
- North of the city on the river at Fyrisfadern: Fyrishov Camping
- South of the city on Lake Ekoln: Sunnersta Camping, off Dag Hammarskjplds vag

Open markets
- Between the river and the cathedral: Saluhallen, an indoor produce market, at Sankt Eriks torg, every day but Sunday
- Behind the railway station, at Valsala torg, every day but Sunday

GOTHENBURG Scandinavia's largest port, this is also one of Sweden's prettiest cities with its pedestrian streets, meandering canals, and colorful gardens.

Special are:
- Spaceport Liseberg. This modern amusement park has gardens, space tower, and restaurants.
- Paddan boat rides through the canals.
- Maritima Centrum. Several ships can be explored. Historic maritime artifacts are exhibited in the museum.

Tourist offices	• At Kungsportsplatsen

• In Nordstan shopping area

Purchasing the Gothenburg card allows the holder admission into all museums, covers public transportation (including canal boat rides), and includes the Liseberg Space Park and public parking. Get the free "Camping Guide for the Swedish West Coast."

Camping places

• On the beach in Askim: Askim Camping
• Close to forests and lakes in Karralunds: Goteborgs Camping Karralund, on Olbergsgatan
• On the beach at Lilleby Havsbad

Open market

In Kungstorget, Stora Saluhallen: an indoor market of baked goods, cheeses, and fish (A fruit and vegetable market is just outside.)

BOHUSLAN

This is a popular holiday area for Swedes along the coast north of Gothenburg. There are lots of camping places, beaches, and bicycling routes.

Special attractions are:

• Kanalmuseum and steep waterfalls at Trollhatten.
• A ferry or bicycle ride along the Gota Canal.
• Mariestad. This small village has a medieval section.
• A cruise up Lake Vanern to the start of the Gota Canal.
• Western buggy peddling on an abandoned railway track along the swimmable river in Gullspang.

MALMO

Malmo is a pretty town with pedestrian streets, flower bedecked squares, half-timbered houses, and a lively atmosphere.

Popular here are:

• Stortorget. This market square goes back to medieval times.
• Lilla Torget. This picturesque, tiny square has half-timbered houses, flowers, oil lamps, and music.
• Malmohus Castle. It has a moat, royal apartments, museums, and galleries.

Tourist office	Across from central station, Skeppsbron 2. "Malmo This Month," city maps, and brochures are free. A Malmo card can be purchased here for museum admissions, parking, guided tours, discounted canal trips, paddle boats, concerts, and cinemas.
Camping place	• In Limhamn past the Limhamn-Dragor ferry terminal, Strandgatan 101
Open markets	• Southern part of Mollevangen, Mollevangstorget, a large produce market, mornings except Sundays
	• At Banerkajen, an early morning fish market, every day but Sunday
	• Fishermen's huts at the canal in front of Malmohus, fish and produce.
	• At Lilla Torg, behind Stortorget, Saluhallen, a large indoor market
LUND	This beautiful university town has an outstanding Romanesque cathedral, medieval museum, and square.
Tourist office	Opposite the cathedral at Klostergatan 11
Camping place	• Southwest of the city: Kallbybadets Camping, off Badarevagen

Lake Siljan Area

Vacationers enjoy this area because of its lush, gentle countryside and the small towns that retain old-fashioned traditions and crafts.

Popular are:

• Open air museums called Gammelgards. Villages are reconstructed, and buildings and homes are furnished in the period. Notable ones are in Rattvik and Mora.

• A huge mine, restored miner's homes, and a museum called Koppargruva. Visitors can go down into the depths of the mine. It is located in Falun.

• Paddling ancient canoes on the lake at Rattvik.

• Bicycling on the Siljansleden, a scenic cycling route.

- Hiking or taking a chair lift to Mickeltemplet for a wonderful view.

Tourist offices   Centrally located in the tourist areas around the lake

Camping places   • Plentiful throughout the area

VISBY ISLAND   Popular with backpackers who have bicycles, this beach town is lively with campers. The walled medieval section houses a castle with a large number of stained glass windows. There is a pleasant botanical garden. Ferry boats go to Faro Island, taking people to see the old steep-pitched reed roofs of the Faro sheepherders.

Tourist office   In the restored half timbered house at Strandgatan 9

Camping places   • Free tent camping at the beach
- On the beach, just outside the city walls: Nordenstrands

VADSTENA   Located on the beautiful Lake Vattern, Vadstena is noted for its Renaissance castle, abbey, and Radhus. Vadstena lace is made and sold here.

Tourist office   In a historic house at Radhustorget

Camping place   • On the lake north of town: Vatterviksbadet

Swedish

Hej da

Hello

Snalla, var ar _____?

Please, where is _____?

Snalla, kan du vanligen skriva.

Please, could you write it down.

Ga rakt fram _____ (meters/kilometers) till _____ (se List Jag Forstar).

Go straight ahead _____ (meters/kilometers) to _____ (see List I Understand).

Forsta svang _____ (hoger/vanster) ga _____ (meters/kilometers) till _____ (se List Jag Forstar).

First turn _____ (right/left) go _____ (meters/kilometers) to _____ (see List I Understand).

Nasta svang _____ (hoger/vanster) ga _____ (meters/kilometers) till _____ (se List Jag Forstar).

Next turn _____ (right/left) go _____ (meters/kilometers) to _____ (see List I Understand).

Hur lang resa? _____ (minuts/timmes)

How long a trip? _____ (minutes/hours)

Tack

Thank you

List I Understand	Liste Jag Forstar
corner	horn
stop sign	stanna
traffic light	trafiksignaler
exit	utgang
road	vag
street	gata
highway	motorvag
large	stor
small	liten
far	fjarran
near	nara
bridge	brygga
river	flod
woods	skog
lake	sjo
harbor	hamm
village	liteu stad
city	stad
house	hus
train station	jarnvagsstation
bus stop	bussen stanna
red	rod
green	gron
blue	bla
yellow	gul
white	vit
black	svart
market place	marknaden
supermarket	specerilagra
gas station	bensinstation
square	torg
main square	stortorget
castle	slott
cathedral	domkyrka
church	kyrkan
camping place	campingplatz
old town	gamla stan
beach	strand
museum	museet

Switzerland

A refined country with awe-inspiring scenery, Switzerland has been an inspiration to well-known artists, writers, and religious and political figures throughout the ages.

The Swiss, both young and old, love to walk and hike. Consequently, they have made it easy to do. You can start in one place and then later be picked up by inexpensive postal bus and taken back to your starting place. There are places on the trails to rest and have light meals and beverages.

Most of the train stations rent bikes that can be dropped off at other train stations.

Best time to go
Switzerland attracts tourists year-round. But for tent camping, late spring, summer, and early fall have the best weather. If you rent a camper van, you can go earlier or later. Changes in weather are frequent, so you'll need to be prepared for rain and cool weather.

Camping places
Camping costs in Switzerland are reasonable compared to staying in hotels and eating in restaurants. However, the camping place fees here compared to those in other countries are high. It is wise to have the international camping carnet card; some camping places require it. (See Appendix: "Documents.") The camping places are clean, well run, and often have extra amenities.

Tourist offices
Tourist offices are marked with a green "i" and are easy to find in tourist areas. Ask for the free maps put out by the Union Bank of Switzerland and the Swiss Bank Corporation. The detailing of streets and sights on these local maps makes getting around much easier.

Food markets
Seek out open markets to stock up on vegetables, fruits, and cheese. Grocery stores are expensive. Bring a cloth bag for transporting your groceries to your car; stores charge for bags.

Hiking
Always carry a waterproof jacket with a hood, even when the weather looks beautiful. It can change dramatically in minutes, and hypothermia is a real threat if you aren't prepared. It's important that you have waterproof headgear to prevent losing body heat. Take a lightweight insulator blanket in a day pack as an extra precaution. Pack some high energy bars, water, and emergency food.

An excellent book which can help you choose the trails that you'll enjoy most:

- Walking Easy in the Swiss Alps, by Chet and Carolee Lipton (800-669-0773)

Driving

Get your International Driver's License before you go. (See Appendix: "Documents.") Gas and tolls are expensive, but the roads are excellent and there are plenty of turnouts for resting or enjoying the scenery. Smaller free roads going over the mountains take much longer and cost more in gas, but the scenery is spectacular. Most main routes have long tunnels. Avoid the small mountain roads unless you have had experience on narrow roads with hairpin turns. Swiss gas is cheaper than French or Italian but about the same as German and Austrian.

Shop hours

Many shops open at 8 A.M. and close at 6:00 P.M. Shops often close for at least an hour for lunch and on Saturdays they generally close earlier. Most stores are closed on Sunday.

BERNE

Located on the Aare River, this is the capital of Switzerland. The altstadt, or old town, boasts beautiful mahogany and sandstone buildings, fountains, bridges, and fine museums. At Helvetiaplatz a one-day ticket can be purchased that permits entry to all the museums located here.

Tourist office

Located in the train station. Get a copy of This Week in Bern to find out about special music and theater productions. Pick up a map to guide you on a pleasant walk through the old town.

Camping places

- South of town near the river: Camping Eichholz
- In Eymatt: Camping Kappelenbrucke

Food markets

- At Barenplatz, mornings
- At Bundesplatz, Tuesdays and Saturdays
- At Waisenhausplatz, Thursdays
  Bernese Oberland

INTERLAKEN

Interlaken is the starting point for adventures in the Bernese Oberland. River rafting, sea kayaking, water-skiing, bungee-jumping, tandem paragliding, and mountain biking are all available for the adventure seeker. The tourist office will help you with arrangements.

Beautiful Wilderswil, just west of Interlaken, is filled with wooden homes in the style of old Switzerland. A cogwheel train goes up to Schynige Platte, where there is a beautiful view and an alpine garden. Seeing the labeled plants here makes identification easier later when hiking. There are excellent hikes throughout the area.

Camping place

- Northwest of Interlaken West: Camp Alpenblick, on Seestrasse by the Lomach River

Jungfrau Region

Breathtaking peaks, waterfalls, glaciers, ice caves, and meadows blanketed with wildflowers are found here. Hiking is excellent.

Camping places

- In Grindelwald, near the Pfingstegg cable car: Camping Gletscherdorf, a wonderful view
- Near Grindelwald Grund, on the other side of the river from Grindelwald: Camping Eigernordwand

Tourist office	In the center of the village, by the Sportzentrum
Camping places	• In Lauterbrunnen, south of the village, on the Panorama walkway toward the falls: Camping Schutzenbach and Camping Jungfrau.

The Lake Region

THUN	Embark here on a leisurely boat trip on the lake to see castles, picturesque villages, and tranquil scenery or indulge in some water sports. The old town is also pleasant.
Tourist office	Just outside the main train station
Camping place	• In Gwatt, on the lake, close to the train station: Camping Betler-reiche
Food market	In the altstadt across the river from the train station, Saturdays
BRIENZ	Brienz is famous for its wood-carving schools. There are tours during the school term, plus an exhibit of finished work. For fine views and trailheads, take the cog-wheel steam train. The Giessbach and Reishenbach Falls and Aare Gorge are close by.
Tourist office	Center of town.
Camping places	• East of the town center, by the lake: Camping Aaregg and Camping Seegartli • Near the Aare Gorge: Camping Aareschult

Ticino—The Italian Switzerland

Located on the southern side of the Alps, Ticino has a warmer climate and less rainfall than other parts of Switzerland. Historically interesting because it played an important position in trade and cultural routes over the centuries, this area has a distinct Mediterranean ambiance.

BELLINZONA   The capital of Ticino, Bellinzona is at the base of two important passes: the San Bernardino and the Gotthard. The town has three well-preserved castles and an excellent open market on Saturdays. The old canton road through the Gotthard Pass is a scenic drive or bike ride. Lake Ritom and the Piora Alpine Park are near Airolo.

Tourist office   At the Palazzo Civico, next to the city hall

Food market   In the historic center, by the tourist office, on Saturdays

Camping place   • North of town in Molinazzo, on the river: Camping Bosco de Molinazzo

LUGANO   Lago di Lugano offers good places to relax in the sun, boat ride, water ski, windsurf, or sail.

Tourist office   Overlooking the lake, at Giocondo Albertolli 5

Camping places   • In Agno, several along the lake

LOCARNO   Situated at the northern end of Lago Maggiore, Locano claims to be warmer than Lugano. Flowers bloom profusely here and Italian piazzas and arcades make for relaxing strolls and people watching. One of the largest film festivals in the world takes place in August in the Piazza Grande.

Val Verzasca, on the old canton road, just north of Locarno, is an especially nice side trip. See the ancient villages of Corippo and Lavertezzo. The spectacular gorges here are popular for swimming in the summer. Easy hiking trails and wine caves (grotti) encourage relaxation.

Tourist office   Close to the Piazza Grande in the Casino Kursaal

Food market   At the Piazza Grande, every other Thursday morning

Camping places   • On the lake: Delta Camping, expensive but lots of amenities

Graubunden

In this area made famous by it resorts—St. Moritz, Arosa, Davos, Klosters, and Flims—tourism is the main industry. Away from the resorts, the terrain is still rugged and unspoiled.

CHUR

The capital of the canton, or "province," this is a nice town to walk around in.

Camping place

• North of town, near the sports center: Camping Au

DAVOS

Originally a health resort, Davos is now also a ski resort. A large collection of the works of Kirchner, the well-known German Expressionist, is housed in the Davos Kirchner Museum. The Davosersee has swimming pools and saunas as well as swimming and fishing. An international classical music festival is held here during July and August.

Camping place

• On the way to Fliuela Pass, just outside of Davos Dorf: Camping Farich

Engadine Valley

MALOJA

Located at the north end of the Engaline Valley and at the southern end of the Maloja pass, this town is a great place for guided hiking trips. The hike from Septimer Pass to Juf is impressive and popular, as is the easier hike to Soglio, a pristine Swiss-Italian village.

Camping place

• In town close to the windsurfing landing: Plan Curtinac

PONTRESINA

Situated close to St. Moritz, this area has excellent hiking. The mountaineering school here offers guided hikes.

Camping place

• Camping Planus

SWISS NATIONAL PARK	Ibexes, chamois, and marmots roam freely in the park. There are also floral gardens with rare specimens.
Camping place	• In Zernez, behind the train station: Camping Cul

Bodensee Area

This popular lake area attracts vacationers from across its three country borders. Dairies and farms dot the countryside. Cheese making and fine textile manufacturing are important industries.

ST. GALLEN	The world-famous Abbey Library (Stiftsbibliotek), which contains an immense collection of ancient manuscripts, is in St. Gallen. Rococo decoration in the baroque reading room is fabulous and worth going out of your way to see. The adjoining cathedral, the Kloster St. Gallen, is considered to be one of the most beautiful in Europe. The old town has many finely restored buildings.
Tourist office	Close to the train station and old town at Bahnhofplatz 1a
Food market	At Marketplatz, mornings, daily
Camping place	• In Wittenbach: Leebrucke, north of town
APPENZELL	This touristy village near St. Gallen has extensive hiking-walking trails dotted with small restaurants. A brewery and narrow-gauge railroad are among the attractions.
STEIN	Cheese-making demonstrations are held in a reconstructed alpine hut here.
Camping place	• In Appenzell: Eischen Camping
ZURICH	Located in central Switzerland, Zurich's national museum, the Schweizerische Landesmuseum, is excellent and provides a good background for travel in the rest of the country. The impressive art museum, Kunsthaus, is one of Switzerland's most important museums. Animal lovers won't want to miss Zoo Dolder—one of the best zoos in the country.

Tourist office
- At the airport in terminal B
- At the Hauptbahnhof at Bahnhofplatz 15

Food market   Near the central streetcar stop, on Saturdays

Camping place
- On the west side of Lake Zurich: Camping Seebucht, Seestrasse 559

WINTERTHUR   Located just northeast of Zurich, Winterthur is worth visiting to see the immense art collection, the Am Romerholz Oskar Reinhart Collection, housed in a beautiful, garden-surrounded villa north of town. Technorama der Schweiz allows you to partake in some hands-on fun and interesting experiments.

Central Switzerland

LUCERNE   Situated picturesquely on the edge of Lake Lucerne, this city has some wonderful museums. The Transport Museum, the Picasso Museum, and the Richard Wagner Museum are worth making a special trip to see. The old town, or altstadt, is impressive with its decorated covered bridge. Boating, kayaking, river rafting, paragliding, and ballooning are available for the energetic and adventurous.

Tourist office   Close to the train station. Take the left exit from the station. It's behind the McDonald's at Frankenstrasse 1. A Short City Guide, listing walking tours, is worth buying. Information about kayaking, river rafting, paragliding, and ballooning is available here.

Food markets   Daily along the quays of the river

Camping place
- East of Lucerne, on the north shore of the lake: Camp Lido

MOUNT PILATUS AND THE RIGI KULM   Check the weather forecast before you book transportation to the peaks of Pilatus and Rigi Kuln. The steepest cogwheel train in the world can take you up Mount Pilatus, or you can take a cable car partway and then do some hiking. For the Rigi Kulm, take the ferry and then the train.

Swiss Jura

BASEL

The countryside is not as spectacular here as in the rest of Switzerland, but the museums and zoo are noteworthy.

Tourist office

On the Rhine River, at the Mittlere Bridge

Food market

At Marketplatz, daily

Camping place

- South of the SBB train station, at Heideweg 16, Reinach: Camping Waldhort

German

Guten tag

Hello

Bitte, wo ist _____?

Please, where is _____?

Konnen sie es bitte aufschreiben.

Could you please write it down.

Gehen Sie geradeaus _____ (meters/kilometers) zu _____ (sehen Liste Ich Verstehe).

Go straight ahead _____ (meters/kilometers) to _____ (show me List I Understand).

Biegen Sie _____ (rechts/links) gehen _____ (meters/kilometers) zu _____ (sehen Liste Ich Verstehe).

Turn _____ (right/left) go _____ (meters/kilometers) to _____ (see List I Understand).

Nachste biegen _____ (rechts/links) gehen _____ (meters/ kilometers) zu _____ (sehen Liste Ich Verstehe).

Next turn _____ (right/left) go _____ (meters/kilometers) to _____ (see List I Understand).

Wie weit ist? _____ (minutes/stundes)

How long will it take? _____ (minutes/hours)

Danke

Thank you

Liste I Understand	Liste Ich Verstehe
corner	ecke
stop sign	stop zeichen
traffic light	stop signal
exit	ausgang
road/street	strade
highway	autostrada
large	gross
small	klein
far	weit
near	nahe
bridge	brucke
river	flub
woods	wald
lake	see
sea	mer
harbor	hafen
village	ort
town/city	stadt
house	haus
train station	bahnhof
bus stop	bushaltestelle
red	rot
green	grun
blue	blau
yellow	geld
white	weiss
black	schwarz
market place	marketplatz
supermarket	supermarket
gas station	benzin
square	platz
main square	haupplatz
castle	schloss
cathedral	Dom
church	kirche
camping place	campingplatz
old town	alstadt
museum	museum

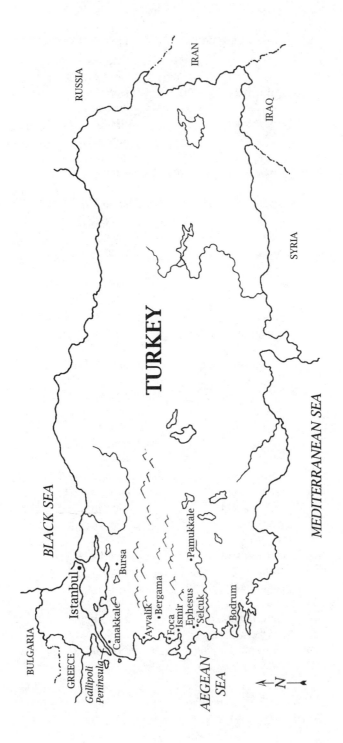

Western Turkey

Graceful Islamic monuments, archaeological treasures, colorful bazaars, stunning coastline, and friendly people await travelers to Turkey.

Highlights are:

- Topkapi Palace. The treasury and the lush haarm is breathtaking.
- Ephesus. The ruins of the largest and best-preserved ancient city on the Mediterranean are very impressive.
- Pamukkale. The snow-white cliffs and thermal-water terraces are alive with color at sunset.
- Bazaars. They are colorful and exotic.
- Ferry cruises. Part of Turkish everyday life, these inexpensive modes of travel are fun.
- Mosques. Colorful mosaic tiles, intricate marble latticework, and graceful architecture make these sacred places special.

When to go

The weather is good in Istanbul and on the Aegean and Mediterranean coasts from April through June and then again in September and October. In July and August the cities and archaeological sites are hot.

Tourist offices

Known as *turizm dernegi,* they are usually located on the main square. English is not readily spoken. Bring maps from home and be sure they have Turkish spellings. Ferry schedules are available at the ferry terminals. Major archaeological sites are open every day from 9 A.M. to 5 P.M. Museums are closed on Mondays.

Camping places

Simple camping places are plentiful and very reasonable. Look for camping signs. Showers are solar heated. Use them in the afternoon when the water is warm. *Pansiyons* (small inexpensive hotels) often allow camping on their property. Bring a plastic shower bag.

Open markets

Food is inexpensive in Turkey because their rich farmlands usually produce a surplus. Coffee is expensive, so bring your own. Good bread, beer, and wine are all inexpensive.

Shop hours	Shops are generally open from 8 A.M. to 5 P.M. everyday but Sunday.
Driving	There are a few expressways and some toll roads, but many of the roads are only two lanes wide. Turks are aggressive drivers, rarely yielding to other cars and often overtaking in unsafe conditions. Leaning on the horn is a common practice. Visitors need to drive defensively, stay levelheaded, and avoid driving at night. Fuel stations are not hard to find. Use the BP, Shell, or Mobil gas stations for better quality gas. Credit cards are often accepted.

Driving

There are a few expressways and some toll roads, but many of the roads are only two lanes wide. Turks are aggressive drivers, rarely yielding to other cars and often overtaking in unsafe conditions. Leaning on the horn is a common practice. Visitors need to drive defensively, stay levelheaded, and avoid driving at night. Fuel stations are not hard to find. Use the BP, Shell, or Mobil gas stations for better quality gas. Credit cards are often accepted.

Take the car ferry, if you face a long stretch of driving, rather than tire yourself on the road. They are inexpensive and convenient, and the scenery and cool breeze make a nice change. Cost for the car on the ferry is about the same as for a passenger. There are sizable discounts for travelers with student or youth cards. Get there early to be sure you get on.

Archaeological signs are black with yellow lettering. Repair shops are easy to find. *Lastikci* means tire.

Make careful notes with the attendant about the rental car's condition when you pick up your vehicle. If damage does occur, get an accident report (*kaza raporu*) from the police station so an insurance claim can be made.

Etiquette

Women should cover their heads before entering a mosque, and both men and women need to have both their legs and upper arms covered. Remove shoes and place on racks inside. Wait thirty minutes after the call to prayer so that prayer is finished for most. Giving a small donation is appropriate. Turks are very patriotic and find insults to Ataturk, or their country, very offensive.

Turkish baths (*Hamams*)

Partaking in this wonderful, inexpensive Turkish custom can make your trip much more enjoyable. There are *hamams* in all towns. Look for a sign or the roof dome. *Erkekler* means men and *kadinlar* means women. Bring your own soap, scrub brush or cloth, shampoo, and shaving supplies. Pay at the front desk according to the posted sign. Store your valuables in a locker and keep the key while you are there. Men are given a wraparound cloth, which they are expected to wear throughout, including when they cleanse the lower half. Women should keep their panties on. Both are given clogs to wear.

The main bath chamber has a raised platform with a warmed bench where customers rest after bathing. Along the sides there are sets of taps and basins. The basin is used for mixing water to the correct temperature, not for mixing water with soap. Use the scoop dishes to get water from the basin to rinse yourself. Be careful not to splash on others because this requires that they clean themselves again. Men shave in the cooling-down room off the main chamber. Its polite to rinse your bench area before leaving.

Ask for a massage from a *tellak* if you would like a vigorous rubdown with an abrasive mitt or *kese*. These mitts can be purchased at a pharmacy, or *eczane*. Agree to the price. It is generally the same price as the basic bath. Tips won't be expected unless you are at a touristed *hamam*.

Eating out

Turkish food is delicious and inexpensive. The street and snack stands have some of the best food in Turkey. Be careful of steam-table food, even though it looks wonderfully inviting. Try to order food that has been freshly cooked for you. It is not necessary to order the whole meal at once. Order as you eat. *Servis dahil* means the tip is included, so just leave some change. *Servis ucreti* means that the service charge is given to the owner, so leave a larger tip of 5 percent or more.

If your stomach is sensitive, have them grill meats well. Drink bottled water, because the local water is heavily chlorinated. Don't eat mussels in the summer. If you have stomach problems, drinks lots of fluids and eat plain rice and yogurt. *Buscopan*, available at the pharmacy, is good for stomach cramps.

ISTANBUL

This three-thousand-year-old exotic city set along the Bosphorus Sea is the heart of Turkish culture.

Tourists enjoy:

- The Grand Bazaar. A maze of color and drama of more that 4,000 shops. Maps are available.

- Topkapi Palace. This is an absolute must. Plan to spend a day enjoying the fabulous treasury, lush rooms of the *haarm*, the huge collection of porcelain and the holy relics. On arrival, get a ticket for the heavily touristed *haarm*, then enjoy the rest of the palace. The beautiful grounds overlook the Bosphorus and Golden Horn. It is closed Tuesdays.

- Ayasofya. Royalty was crowned in this ancient sanctuary, now a museum. An architectural wonder for its day, it was once the greatest church in Christendom. Enter through the front doors and proceed slowly to appreciate each part.

- Blue Mosque. The silhouette of six minarets, the intricate marble latticework, and the blue Iznik tile interior are magnificent. Enter from the front.
- Turkish and Islamic Arts Museum. Housed in the sixteenth-century Palace of Ibrahim, this is a good first stop. The video show on the first floor gives a quick synopsis of Turkish history. There is an excellent collection of Turkish carpets and Islamic artifacts with English labels.
- Ferry cruises on the Bosphorus. They leave from Pier 3.
- Egyptian spice bazaar. This is where locals buy snacks, sweets, aphrodisiacs, and spices. It is less touristy than other areas.
- Dolmabahce Palace. Elegantly located on the Bosphorus, this extravagantly built and furnished palace was home for the Ottoman sultans in the 1800s.
- Yidiz palace and park. A delightful summer palace built in the late 1800s, it has housed the famous since then.
- Yerebatan cistern. An underground cavern with 336 columns and wooden walkways, it is enhanced by atmospheric lighting and music.
- Suleymaniye Camii. This is the largest mosque. Its size and simplicity are awe inspiring.
- Galata tower. The view is fabulous. Walk across the Galata Bridge and then take the Tunel, a very short train ride, to the top of the hill.

Tourist offices
- At Ataturk airport
- At the north end of the Hippodrome near the Blue Mosque
- In the Hilton Hotel arcade in Taksim on the north side of the Golden Horn

Camping places
- All close to the airport, along the Marmara coast, near the highway to Istanbul (There is public transport to the city center.)

Open market
- At Altiyol in Kadikoy, called *Sali Pazari,* Tuesdays and Fridays
- Next to the Egyptian spice market, mainly fresh fruit
- Next to Cicek Pasaji, in Beyoglu, called *Balik Pazari*
- In residential neighborhoods, called *Halk Pazari*

BURSA

An ancient city, set beneath the slopes of Mount Uludag, it was once the capital of the Ottoman empire and famous for its thermal baths and silk trade. It now is an industrial center with an interesting history.

Be sure to see:

- Yesil Camii. The pure Turkish architecture of this mosque is exquisite. It is called the Green Mosque; the rich tile work is turquoise. The sultan's lavish residence is on the side.
- Yesil Turbe. Close to the mosque, these tombs are also beautifully tiled. There are wonderful panoramic views.
- Beyazit Camii. This is a mosque has two domes.
- Bat Pazari. This colorful marketplace is great for photographing.
- Bedesten. In this covered market you'll find the shadow puppets that Bursa made popular. Koza Han, where silkworms are traded, is just outside the eastern entrance.
- Cumali Kizik. This authentic Ottoman era domestic village, just outside of town, is protected from development.

Tourist office

North entrance to Orhan Gazi Atgecidi pedestrian underground walkway, across from a small park

Camping places

- On the Yalova road, several

Open market

South of Ulu Camii, in Tahtakale/Inebey district

CANAKKALE

People come here to see the Gallipoli (*Gelibolu*) war sites and the ruins of Troy. It is militarily a historic site; in 480 B.C. Xerxes' Persian soldiers crossed the Dardanelles on their way to Greece. Today people come mainly to see the battlefields where both Allied and Turk troops suffered tremendous losses. If you are viewing the battlefield, tours are helpful. Down Under Travel Agency, near the small town of Ecebat, has good prices. (Be sure your guide speaks good English before starting out.)

Also note:

- ANZAC House Cafe in Yellow Rose Pension is a meeting place for campers of all nationalities. It shows the film Gallipoli and the documentary Fatal Shore daily.
- The dawn ceremony at ANZAC cove pays tribute to those who lost their lives.

- The Naval Museum houses interesting photos and memorabilia of Ataturk and the battles.
- The Nusrat replica shows the famous minelayer used for picking up loose mines at night and re-laying them.
- Truva displays nine layers of remains that span 4,000 years.

Tourist office   Next to the main dock, close to the clock tower (pick up free maps of the battlefields.)

Camping places
- South of town in Kepez
- Southwest of town on the road to Truva in the beach town of Guzelyali
- On the Gallipoli Peninsula, south of Kabatepe in Kum Limani

AYVALIK   This is a pleasant place to stay while visiting the important Hellenistic ruins in Bergama. This beach town, just across from the Greek island of Lesbos, produces olive oil and soap. A small, pleasant island just across from Ayvalik and linked by a causeway has picturesque seaside cafes and camping.

In Bergama see:
- The Archaeology Museum.
- The Acropolis with its immense library, theater, and temple.
- The ancient medical center or Asciepion.
- The Red Basilica or Kizil Avlu.

Tourist office   South of the main square, on the road to Sarimasakli, across from the yacht harbor

Camping places
- At the beach, south of town at Sarimsakli Plaj
- On the island of Alibey Adasi
- Just out of Bergama, east of the highway junction

Open market
- In Ayvalik, several streets back from the waterfront; known for its cheese, bread, and yogurt; every day but Sunday (On Thursdays the market is bigger.)
- In Bergama, in the small plaza by the Red Basilica

FOCA

This small fishing port is a popular beach town for middle-class Turks. There are lovely coves in the area that have sandy beaches.

Camping places

Along the coastline

ISMIR

This major port is the third largest city in Turkey. The Ethnology Museum here houses interesting displays of Turkish culture, history, and crafts. The bazaar is colorful. Sardis, the ancient village with important Roman and Byzantine ruins, is close by.

Tourist office

Between the train and ferry terminal at Alsancak Cad 418

Camping places

- On the road to Cesme: OBA Dinleme Tesisleri, Guzelbahce
- West of Konak: BP Mocamp, Inciralti

EPHESUS

One of the largest and best preserved ancient cities on the Mediterranean, it shouldn't be missed when visiting Turkey.

Besides the fabulous ruins, see:

- Ephesus Museum. In Secuk, go here first before visiting the ruins.
- St. John Basilica. St. John is reputed to have written his epistle here.
- Meryemania. Set among the pines on a hilltop, it is thought to be a home for the Virgin Mary.
- Priene, Miletus, and Didyma. These important settlements include an outstanding theater and temple. There is camping in the area.

Tourist office

In Selcuk, opposite the bus terminal and close to the museum on the south side of the park

Camping places

- In Selcuk, west side of Ayasoluk Hill, just beyond the Isabey Camii: Garden Motel and Camping
- On the beach in Pamucak
- On the beach north of the resort town of Kusadasi
- Inland from the yacht harbor at Kusadasi

PAMUKKALE   The snow-white cliffs formed over the millennia from calcium deposited by the thermal springs are known locally as Cotton Castle. Mineral water collects on the terraces and forms pools. At sunset the area glows with pink, purple, and gold. Enjoy the mineral water at the garden pool of Pamukkale Motel, where ancient columns from the Roman baths are submerged.

Tourist office   On the way to the Pamukkale Motel

Camping places   • Near the bus station: Rose Pansiyon and Camping
• On the road to Karahayit: Mistur Motel and Camping
• On the road from Denizli

BODRUM   At this beautiful seaside resort, white-washed houses, yachts, and discos are popular. There is an interesting display of a large shipwreck at the Museum of Archaeology.

Tourist office   On the main square beneath the castle walls

Open market   Close to the bus station (*otogar*) and small mosque, Thursdays and Fridays

Camping places   • On Gumbet Beach, just outside of Bodrum: Zeta's Camping
• In Yalikavak, on the north end of the peninsula: Yali Camping, at the harbor

Western Mediterranean Coast

Popular with yacht owners, this coastline of beautiful, secluded coves and seaside villages is spectacular.

Popular attractions are:

- Yacht cruises or day boat excursions.
- Sunning and swimming.
- Exploring ancient ruins.

Tourist offices　On the main square or close to the harbor. Book boat trips at the dock. Check the daily itinerary and what is on the menu. Haggling on the ticket price is acceptable.

Camping places　• Drive along the coast and look for camping signs. Because the area is changing rapidly due to tourism, camping places change locations. Ask to camp at the *pansiyons*.

Open markets　Just off the main square, on the side streets

Turkish

Merhaba

Hello

Lutfen, _____ nerede?

Please, _____ is where?

Yazmak kaydetmek, lutfen.

Write it down, please.

Direk _____ (meters/kilometers) e _____ (gormek Liste Anlamak).

Straight ahead _____ meters/kilometers) to _____ (see List I Understand).

Ilk don _____ (sag/sol) baslamak _____ (meters/kilometers) e _____ (gormek Liste Anlamak).

First turn _____ (right/left) go _____ (meters/kilometers) to _____ (see List I Understand).

En yakin don _____ (Sag/sol) baslamak _____ (meters/kilometers) e _____ (gormek Liste Anlamak).

Next turn _____ (right/left) go _____ (meters/kilometers) to _____ (see List I Understand).

Kac surer? _____ (dakika/saat)

How long will it take? _____ (minutes/hours)

Sa gol

Thank you

List I Understand	Liste Anlamak
intersection	kesismek
stop sign	durmak isaret
traffic light	trafik hafif
exit	cikis
road	yol
street	cadde
highway	anayol
large	buyuk
small	ufak
far	uzak
near	yakin
bridge	kopru
river	irmak
woods	orman
lake	go
sea	deniz
harbor	liman
village	koy
town	kasaba
city	sehir
house	ev
train station	tren durak
bus stop	otobus durmak
red	kirmizi
green	yesil
blue	mavi
yellow	sari
white	beyaz
black	siyah
market place	pazar
grocery store	bakkal
gas station	gaz dukkan
castle	kale
cathedral	katedral
church	kilise
camping place	kamp
turkish bath	hamam
beach	plaj

Appendix

Using Public Transportation

Have the camping place office write down the name of your destination stop and the name of your return stop. Show the name to a fellow passenger and ask the person to tell you where to get off. Use the fill-in forms at the end of each country, for asking people for further directions to your destination.

Tourist Offices

After getting settled in your camping place, always make the tourist office your next stop. You can get information about other camping places, food markets, walking tours, and current productions in music, dance, and theater, as well as have information on hiking, river rafting, and kayaking.

Food Markets

Organize your shopping around open markets. They are inspiring and economical.

Buying Gas

The cheapest gas is often found in stations on roads that lead out of town or that are close to a large supermarket rather than along the autostratas. Pumps with green stripes commonly indicate unleaded gas. Leaded gas is often called Regular or Normal, while leaded super is called Super. Write down the name of the type of gas you need when you pick up your vehicle.

Parking

Look at the parked vehicles in the area you want to park. Then follow suit. If you see tickets displayed that indicate payment for an amount of time, look for a machine in the area that dispenses tickets. If you see discs displayed that show time, these can be obtained from the vehicle rental office on your arrival. A parking disc might be with the car documents. Set the hands of the disc to show your arrival time. These parking areas are called Blue Zones. The discs are free and so is the limited time parking. Observe stickers that indicate that parking is for residents only.

Road Signs

Red indicates negative, prohibitive, or warning information. Blue indicates positive information, such as rest stops or bicycle paths. Names of roads or streets are frequently posted on buildings.

Border Crossing

Crossing borders is usually easy. Many countries don't check at all. Sometimes you will need to slow down and show your passport. Be sure to keep the car registration and insurance papers easily accessible.

Avoiding Burglary from Your Vehicle

Try to make your vehicle look as though a local owns it. Thieves know that tourists carry more valuables in their vehicles.

Also take the following precautions:

- Cover all car rental advertising with stickers from the country you are traveling in.
- Put out of sight anything that shows you speak English and anything you don't want stolen.
- Park where a break-in would be noticed by traffic or pedestrians.
- In an attended parking area, park where your vehicle can be seen by the attendant.
- Be extra careful in tourist areas. This is where thieves work.

Vehicle Insurance

Before taking the insurance that the rental company offers, check with several other insurance carriers. Also check with both the company that covers you currently and the credit card company you'll be using for renting the vehicle. Travel Guard Insurance (1-800-782-5151, 1145 Clark Street, Stevens Point, WI 54481), is a good resource. Always ask for and make note of the name of the person with whom you are talking, because that makes the call friendlier and provides a reference for future calls and correspondence.

Find out:

- Does the company insure drivers who are renting and driving in Europe?
- Which European countries does the company cover?
- What is the deductible?
- How many consecutive days is the insurance valid? (Some policies are for fourteen consecutive days only.)
- What is the cost of an additional driver?
- Does the insurance include collision (CDW) or theft (LDW)?
- Is there a minimum or maximum age limit?
- Does the coverage include at-fault drivers?

Your existing insurance might cover some of the above. Compare the information you gather with the vehicle rental company's policy.

Renting Your Vehicle

To secure the best terms, reserve before you leave. Personalize and document your reservation by asking the name of the person with whom you are talking. Auto Europe claims they will beat any offer, so call some other companies before you call them.

Establish:

- Type of vehicle you want to rent.
- Cost, including tax but without insurance, for the number of days you need.
- Cancellation or alteration fees.
- Insurance costs. Get documentation of all the points outlined in the Appendix: "Vehicle Insurance."
- How much mileage is included.
- Pick up and return locations.
- Additional driver charges.
- Service and timeliness of the repair or replacement of a vehicle.
- Partial refund on VAT and the procedure for getting it, if you are driving in a country that has a lower VAT than the country where you are picking up your vehicle.

Get a written guarantee of all the above quotations both when you are doing your research and in the final reservation contract.

International Vehicle Rental Companies

Alamo: 800-522-9696

Auto Europe: 800-223-5555

Avis: 800-331-1084

Budget: 800-472-3325

Dollar: 800-800-6000

Hertz: 800-654-3000

Kemwel: 800-678-0678

International Camper Van Rental Companies

U.S. Companies Renting in Western Europe	Auto Europe 1-800 223-5555
	Avis 1-800-331-1084
	Bon Voyage by Car 1-800-272-3299
	Hertz Auto Rental 1-800-654-3001
Denmark	Camperudlejning Copenhagen 53-64-34-52
	RAFCO Copenhagen 45-31-51-15-00
Greece	Camper Caravans Athens 1-32-30-55-25
	Galatoulas Company Motor Caravans Club Haidari 1-58-12-103
Italy	Freedom Holiday Rome 6-60-94-212
	Rome Camper Rome 6-64-81-504
	Campernolo Milan 23-22-667
	Central Camping Florence 55-372336
Netherlands	Lokhorst Autoverhuur Amsterdam 35-21-73-33
	Tigchelaar Recreatie Amsterdam 76-28-14-81
	KAV Auto Verhuur Amsterdam 20-69-69-730
Norway	Gumpens Auto Stockholm 42-29-590
	Auto Camping Bergen 5-24-05-38
Poland	Americana Rent-A-Car Warsaw 25-72-75
Portugal	Delta Car Lisbon 1-84-81-428
	Dias & Santos Lisbon 1-87-31-91
Spain	Camper Europa Madrid 1-56-28-270
	Caravan Travel Madrid 1-65-40-249
Turkey	Europcar Autovermietung 40-52-01-28-11
	Global Transport Tourisik 60-39-43-011 (book in Germany; pick up in Turkey)

Document Information

Passport

You need a valid passport to enter any European country. It must be valid through your return trip. You will also need it to change money or traveler's checks. Apply in person at a passport agency or main post office. You must have with you: two passport photos, your birth certificate, and photo identification.

Visa

You won't need a visa to travel in Western Europe but check current requirements for traveling in Eastern Europe and Turkey.

International Driving Permit (IDP)

This document repeats the information on your domestic driver's license with legends in several languages; enabling officials to read your license. To get one, call your local auto club. You will need two passport photos. Your international driver's permit is valid only in conjunction with your domestic license. Keep both readily available.

International Student Identity Card (ISIC)

Card holders are entitled to discounts on sightseeing and some transportation. Apply through a student union.

Federal International Youth Travel Organization Card (FIYTO)

Card holders are entitled to discounts on sightseeing and some transportation. Apply through a youth hostel organization.

Senior Citizen Card

Membership entitles you to discounts on sightseeing and some transportation. Apply through a senior organization.

United States: American Association of Retired Persons (AARP), 800-927-0111

International Camping Carnet Card

Membership in a camping organization that distributes these cards covers you for liability for property damage and personal injury caused at a camping place. Some camping places require it. You can also opt to leave this card, instead of your passport, with the camping place office during your stay.

To obtain the card contact:

United States: Family Campers and RVers Association, 716-668-6242, fax same

Britain: Caravan Club: 342-32 69 44, fax 342-41 02 58

Canada: National Campers and Hikers Association, 416-385-1866

Resources

Maps

Michelin Travel Publications:
   United States: 803-458-6470, fax 803-458-6630
   Canada: 514-636-5920, fax 514-636-6828
   Britain: 81-861-2121, fax 81-863-0680

Recommended General Budget Guide Books

Let's Go guides: 800-221-7945, fax 617-496-8015
Lonely Planet guides: 800-275-8555, fax 510-893-8563
Rough or Real guides: 800-253-6476, fax 201-385-6521

Camping Equipment

REI (Recreational Equipment, Inc.) 800-426-4840 for catalog and store locations

Average Weekly Auto Rental Rates

Country	Cheapest	Cheapest Automatic	Compact	Midsize
Austria	$234	$486	$254	$433
Belgium	130	258	134	205
Czech Republic	309	574	313	485
Denmark	279	644	302	445
France	309	575	313	485
Germany	134	287	146	212
Greece	236	578	334	439
Hungary	292	377	301	460
Italy	313	601	335	549
Netherlands	193	313	204	343
Norway	344	643	352	524
Poland	321	1185	352	549
Portugal	162	388	175	413
Spain	206	425	207	423
Switzerland	167	287	178	257
Turkey	357	—	361	589

Figures include VAT (Value Added Tax), unlimited mileage, and an average rate between high and low season. They do not include CDW (Collision Damage Waiver) or airport surcharges. Figures are based on Spring 1996 rates and are subject to change.

Temperatures and Rainfall

	Jan	Feb	Mar	Apr	May	Jun	Jul	Aug	Sep	Oct	Nov	Dec
Vienna, Austria												
high (°F)	34	38	47	57	66	71	75	73	66	55	44	37
prec. (in.)	1.5	1.4	1.8	2.0	2.8	2.7	3.0	2.7	2.0	2.0	1.9	1.8
Prague, Czechoslovakia												
high (°F)	34	38	45	55	65	72	74	73	65	54	41	34
prec. (in.)	09	0.8	1.1	1.5	2.4	2.8	2.6	2.2	1.7	1.2	1.2	0.9
Copenhagen, Denmark												
high (°F)	36	36	41	50	61	67	72	69	63	53	43	38
prec. (in.)	1.6	1.3	1.2	1.7	1.7	2.1	2.2	3.2	1.9	2.1	2.2	2.1
Nice, France												
high (°F)	56	56	59	64	69	76	81	81	77	70	62	58
prec. (in.)	2.4	2.4	3.2	1.9	2.8	1.0	0.7	1.3	3.0	4.5	5.6	3.5
Paris, France												
high (°F)	56	56	59	64	69	73	75	75	69	59	49	43
prec. (in.)	1.5	1.3	1.5	1.7	2.0	2.1	2.1	2.0	2.0	2.2	2.0	1.9
Frankfurt, Germany												
high (°F)	37	42	49	58	67	72	75	74	67	56	45	39
prec. (in.)	1.7	1.3	1.6	1.5	2.0	2.5	2.8	2.6	1.9	2.2	2.0	2.0
Munich, Germany												
high (°F)	34	38	47	57	66	71	75	73	66	55	44	37
prec. (in.)	1.5	1.4	1.8	2.0	2.8	2.7	3.0	2.7	2.0	2.0	1.9	1.8
Athens, Greece												
high (°F)	54	55	60	67	77	85	90	90	83	74	64	57
prec. (in.)	2.2	1.6	1.4	0.8	0.8	0.6	0.2	0.4	1.6	1.7	2.8	2.8

Temperatures and Rainfall

	Jan	Feb	Mar	Apr	May	Jun	Jul	Aug	Sep	Oct	Nov	Dec
Budapest, Hungary												
high (°F)	35	40	51	62	72	78	82	81	74	61	47	38
prec. (in.)	1.5	1.5	1.7	2.0	2.7	2.6	2.0	1.9	1.8	2.1	2.4	2.0
Rome, Italy												
high (°F)	34	38	47	57	66	71	75	73	66	55	44	37
prec. (in.)	1.5	1.4	1.8	2.0	2.8	2.7	3.0	2.7	2.0	2.0	1.9	1.8
Venice, Italy												
high (°F)	43	46	54	63	71	78	82	82	78	56	54	46
prec. (in.)	1.6	1.8	2.0	1.6	3.2	2.6	2.8	1.7	2.4	3.4	3.1	2.4
Amsterdam, Netherlands												
high (°F)	40	41	46	52	60	65	69	68	64	56	47	41
prec. (in.)	2.0	1.4	1.3	1.6	1.8	1.8	2.6	2.7	2.8	2.8	2.6	2.2
Bergen, Norway												
high (°F)	43	44	47	55	64	70	72	70	64	57	49	45
prec. (in.)	7.9	6.0	5.4	4.4	3.9	4.2	5.2	7.3	9.9	9.2	8.0	8.1
Oslo, Norway												
high (°F)	30	32	40	50	62	69	73	69	60	49	37	31
prec. (in.)	1.7	1.3	1.4	1.6	1.8	2.4	2.9	3.8	2.5	2.9	2.3	2.3
Warsaw, Poland												
high (°F)	30	32	41	54	67	72	75	73	65	54	40	32
prec. (in.)	1.2	1.1	1.3	1.5	1.9	2.6	3.0	3.0	1.9	1.7	1.4	1.4
Lisbon, Portugal												
high (°F)	56	58	61	64	69	75	79	80	76	69	62	57
prec. (in.)	3.3	3.2	3.1	2.4	1.7	0.7	0.2	0.2	1.4	3.1	4.2	3.6

Temperatures and Rainfall

	Jan	Feb	Mar	Apr	May	Jun	Jul	Aug	Sep	Oct	Nov	Dec
Barcelona, Spain												
high (°F)	56	57	61	64	71	77	81	82	78	71	62	57
prec. (in.)	1.2	2.1	1.9	1.8	1.8	1.3	1.2	1.7	2.6	3.4	2.7	1.8
Madrid, Spain												
high (°F)	47	51	57	64	71	80	87	86	77	66	54	48
prec. (in.)	1.1	1.7	1.7	1.7	1.5	1.2	0.4	0.3	1.2	1.9	2.2	1.6
Stockholm, Sweden												
high (°F)	31	31	37	45	57	65	70	66	58	48	38	33
prec. (in.)	1.5	1.1	1.1	1.6	1.9	2.8	3.1	2.1	2.1	1.9	1.9	1.9
Zurich, Switzerland												
high (°F)	36	41	52	60	67	73	77	76	70	57	45	36
prec. (in.)	1.9	2.2	3.0	3.8	4.5	5.3	5.2	5.2	4.3	4.1	2.8	2.9

Index

A

Abbeys
France, Saint Michel in
Mont St.-Michel, 92–
93
Hungary
Benedictine in Tihany,
125
Italy, Abbey di Sant' Anti-
mo in Montalcino,
138
Spain, Monestir Poblet in
Tarragonia, 190
Sweden, Vadstena, 205
Switzerland, Abbey Li-
brary (Stiftsbib-
liotek) in St. Gallen,
215
See also Monasteries
Accidents, reporting
Czech and Slovak Repub-
lics, 59
Norway, 156
Sweden, 200
Western Turkey, 222
Acropolis, Athens, Greece,
110
Agora, Athens, Greece, 110
Airplane, boarding, 18–20
reservations, 8–9
Aix en Provence, France, 88
Alamo, International Vehicle
Rental, 236
Alcobaca, Portugal, 179
Al dente, defined, 46

Algarve, Portugal, 178
Alsace-Lorraine Area, France,
91–92
Amalfi Coast, Italy, 140
Amsterdam
Netherlands, 149
average temperatures
and rainfall, 241
Amusement parks
Denmark, Tivoli in Copen-
hagen, 70
Sweden, Gothenburg,
Spaceport Lise-
berg, 202
Ancient ruins
Greece
Athens, 110
Crete, 113
Delphi, 111
Epidaurus, 112
Kos, 115
Mycenae, 112
Mystra, 112
Olympia, 112
Rhodes, 114
Samothrace, 115
Santorini (Thira), 117
Hungary
Visegrad, 123
Italy
Pompeii, Herculane-
um, 140
Rome, 132
Norway, Bergen, 160
Spain, Castell de Morella,
192

Turkey
Ayvalik, 226
Ephesus, 227
Truva, 226
Andulusia, Spain, 193–194
Appenzell, Switzerland, 215
Aquariums, Norway, Bergen,
160
Aqueducts, Spain, Aqueducto
Romano in Segovia,
188
Arhus, Denmark, 74
Arles, France, 87
"Asking for Directions" forms
Austria, 55
Czech/Slovak, 66
Denmark, 76
France, 95
Germany, 106
Greece, 118
Hungary, 128
Italy, 145
Netherlands, 152
Norway, 163
photocopying, 11
Poland, 172
Portugal, 182
Spain, 195
Sweden, 206
Switzerland, 218
using, 5, 27
Western Turkey, 230
Assisi, Italy, 133
Athens, Greece, 110–111
average temperatures and
rainfall, 242

Aurlandsfjord, Norway, 161
Auschwitz, Poland, 169
Austria, 48–56
 temperatures and rainfall, 241
 Weekly Auto Rental Rates, 240
Auto Europe
 International Camper Van Rental, 237
 International Vehicle Rental, 236
Avignon, France, 87
Avis
 International Camper Van Rental, 237
 International Vehicle Rental, 236
Ayvalik, Western Turkey, 226

B

Backpacking, Sweden, Visby Island, 205
Baden-Baden, Germany, 102
Baden-Wurttemberg Area, Germany, 102
Balatonfured, Hungary, 125
Balaton Lake, Hungary, 124
Baleraric Islands, Spain, 192
Ballooning, Switzerland, Luc- erne, 216
Barcelona, Spain, 189–190
 average temperatures and rainfall, 243
Bartok, home of, 121
Basel, Switzerland, 217
Basque country
 France, 90–91
 Spain, 194
Bavarian Alps, Germany, 101
Bavarian Forest (Bayerischer Wald), Germany, 102
Bavarian region, Germany, 100
Bayeux, France, 93
Bayonne, France, 90
Bazaars, Western Turkey
 Egyptian spice in Istanbul, 224
 Grand Bazaar in Instanbul, 223
 Ismir, 227

Beaches
 Denmark
  Hornbaek, 73
  Marielyst, 73
 France
  Concarneau, 94
  Saint Malo, 94
 Greece
  Island of Samothrace, 115
  Island of Skiathos, 116
  Island of Zakynthos, 116
 Hungary
  Balaton Lake, 124
  Siofok, 124
 Italy
  Almalfi, 140
  Lido, 143
  Marche, 138
  Northern Italy, 140
 Netherlands, Haarlem, 150
 Norway, Kristansand, 162
 Poland, Pomerania, 170
 Portugal
  The Algarve, 178
  West of Lisbon, 177
 Spain
  Baleraric Islands, 192
  Costa Brava, 191
  La Concha in San Sa- bastian, 194
 Sweden
  Bohuslan, 203
  Lake Siljan Area, 204– 205
 Western Turkey
  Ayvalik, 226
  Bodrum, 228
  Foca, 227
  Western Mediterra- nean Coast, 229
Beaune, France, 85
Beer, home of Budweiser, 62
Beer halls
 Austria, Salzburg, 50
 Czech Republic, U Fleku in Prague, 61
 Germany, Frankfurt, 104
Beethoven, home of, 51
Bellinzona, Switzerland, 213
Berlenga Island, Portugal, 179

Berlin, Germany, average tem- peratures and rain- fall, 241
Berne, Switzerland, 210
Biarritz, France, 90
Bicycle
 accessories, 16
 assembly, 19–20
 packing, 1, 13
 timing arrival and depar- ture, 18–19
Biking
 Austria
  Salzkammerg Ut Re- gion, 51
  Vienna, 51
 Denmark, 69–70
  Jutland, 74
 France, 80
  Beaune, 85
  Britagne, 93–94
  Loire Valley, 83
  Quimper, 93
 Germany
  Cologne, 105
  Danube River Area, 103
  in general, 99
  Lake Constance (Bod- ensee), 103
  Munich, 100
 Hungary, in general, 121
 Netherlands
  in general, 149
  Haarlem, 150
 Norway, Lillehammer, 159
 Poland, 167
 Portugal, 175
 Spain, Baleraric Islands, 192
 Sweden
  Bohuslan, 203
  in general, 199
  Siljansleden, 204
 Switzerland
  Bellinzona, 213
  in general, 209
  Interlaken, 211
Birkenau, Poland, 169
Black Forest (Schwarzwald), Germany, 103
Black Madonna, Poland, Jas- na Gora in Czesto- chowa, 170

Black Virgin Mary, Spain,
Montserrat, 190
Blois, France, 84
Boating
Greece, Zakynthos, Blue
Caves, 116
Poland, Gdansk, 171
Portugal, Berlinga Island,
179
Spain
Baleraric Islands, 192
Costa Brava, 191
Sweden, Gothenburg, 202
Switzerland
Lucerne, 216
Lugano, 213
Thun, 212
Turkey, Western Mediter-
rean Coast, 229
Bodensee Area, Switzerland,
215–216
Bodrum, Western Turkey, 228
Bohemia, Czech and Slovak
Republics, 60–63
Bohuslan, Sweden, 203
Bonaparte, Napoleon, site of
defeat, 63
Bon Voyage by Car, Interna-
tional Camper Van
Rental, 237
Books, foreign language
phrase, 11
Bordeaux Region, France, 89–
90
Border crossings, documenta-
tion needed, 234
Brahms, home of, 51
Braise, defined, 46
Braising, technique, 33
Bratislava, Czech Republic, 65
Breweries
Czech Republic, Urqueil
in Plzen, 62
Denmark
Carlsberg in Copen-
hagen, 71
Ceres in Arhus, 74
Switzerland, Appenzell,
215
Brienz, Switzerland, 212
Britagne Area, France, 93–94
Brno, Czech Republic, 63

Broccoli
with potatoes and onions,
38
with red peppers and ol-
ives, 37
Brussels, Belgium, average
temperature and
rainfall, 241
Budapest, Hungary, 122
average temperatures and
rainfall, 242
Budget, International Vehicle
Rental, 236
Bugac, Hungary, 126
Buggy peddling, Sweden, Bo-
huslan, 203
Buildings
Czech and Slovak Repub-
lics, Dom Odborov
in Bratislava, 65
France
Hotel-Dieu in Beaune,
85
Pantheon in Paris, 81
Germany, Dom in Co-
logne, 105
Greece, third century the-
ater in Epidaurus,
112
Hungary, Katona theater
in Kecskemet, 126
Italy
Duomo in Milan, 142
Duomo in Orivieto, 135
Piza, 138
Norway, Tryvannstarnet
Tower in Oslo, 157
Portugal, Temple of Diana
in Evora, 179
Spain, La Granja near Seg-
ovia, 188
See also Structures
Bullfights
Portugal, 175-176
Spain, Sevilla, 193
Bungee-jumping, Switzerland,
Interlaken, 211
Burglary
avoiding vehicle, 235
securing yourself against,
5
Burgundy Area, France, 85–86
Bursa, Western Turkey, 225

Butterflies, Valley of, Pataloudes, Greece, 116

C

Cable cars
Austria, Salzkammerg Ut
Region, 51
France, French Alps, 86
Germany, Garmisch-
Partenkirchen, 101
Italy, Gran Sasso, 139
Poland, Zakopane, 168
Switzerland, Mount Pila-
tus, 216
Camper Carnet Card, 239
Camper vans, familarization,
21
Camping equipment, resourc-
es, 239
Camping places
Austria
general info, 49
Hallstatt, 51
Innsbruck, 52
Kitzbuhel, 54
Lechtaler Alps, 53
Leinz, 54
Salzburg, 50
Salzburger Sportwelt
Amade, 51
Salzkammerg Ut Re-
gion, 51
Vienna, 52
Zell am Zeller, 54
Czech and Slovak Repub-
lics, in general, 59
Czech Republic
Bratislava, 65
Brno, 63
Ceske Budejovice, 62
Karlovy Vary, 61
Plzen, 62
Prague, 61
Slovakia, 64
Denmark
Arhus, 74
Copenhagen, 71
in general, 69
Helsingor, 72
Hillerod, 72
Odense, 73
Ribe, 74
Romo, 75
Roskilde, 73

Zealand, 73
finding, 27
France
  Aix en Provence, 88
  Arles, 87
  Avignon, 87
  Bayeux, 93
  Bayonne, 90
  Beaune, 85
  Biarritz, 91
  Blois, 84
  Bordeaux, 90
  Cauterets, 91
  Chamonix, 86
  Colmar, 92
  Concarneau, 94
  Cote d'Azur (French
    Riveria), 88–89
  Dijon, 85
  in general, 79
  Giverny, 82
  Grenoble, 86
  Lyon, 85
  Menton, 89
  Mont St.-Michel, 93
  Nancy, 92
  Nice, 89
  Normandy area, 92–93
  Orleans, 83
  Paris, 82
  Quimper, 93
  Saint Malo, 94
  Strasbourg, 92
Germany
  Baden-Baden, 102
  Black Forest, 103
  Cologne, 105
  Danube River Area, 103
  Frankfurt, 104
  Garmisch-Partenkirch-
    en, 101
  in general, 99
  Heidelberg, 102
  Lake Constance (Bod-
    ensee), 103
  Munich, 100
  Nuremberg, 100
  Rhineland, 104
  Stuttgart, 102
  Zwiesel, 102
Greece
  Athens, 110
  Delphi, 111–112
  Epidaurus, 112

  in general, 109
  Hania, Crete, 114
  Iraklion, Crete, 113
  Island of Corfu, 115
  Island of Folegandros,
    117
  Island of Kos, 115
  Island of Mykonos, 116
  Island of Paros, 116–
    117
  Island of Patmos, 115
  Island of Rhodes, 114
  Island of Samothrace,
    115
  Island of Skiathos, 116
  Island of Thira (Santori-
    ni), 117
  Island of Tilos, 114
  Island of Zakynthos,
    116
  Mycenae, 112
  Mystra, 112
  Olympia, 112
  Phaestos, Crete, 113
Hungary
  Aggtelek National Park,
    127
  Balatonfured, 125
  Budapest, 122
  Eger, 127
  Esztergom, 123
  in general, 121
  Kecskemet, 126
  Keszthely, 125
  Pecs, 125
  Siofok, 124
  Sopron, 124
  Szeged, 126
  Szentendre, 123
  Tokaj, 127
Italy
  Amalfi Coast, 140
  Assisi, 133
  Dolomites and South
    Tyrol, 142
  Florence, 137
  in general, 131
  Genoa, 140
  Gran Paradiso National
    Park, 141
  Gran Sasso, 139
  Gubbio, 134
  Lago di Como, 144
  Lago di Garda, 143–144

  Lago di Maggiore, 144
  Lago Trasimeno, 134
  Lucca, 138
  Marche, 139
  Milan, 142
  Montalcino, 138
  National Park of Abruz-
    zo, 140
  Orivieto, 135
  Pergugia, 133
  Piza, 138
  Pompeii, Herculaneum
    and Mt. Vesuvius,
    140
  Rivera di Ponente, 141
  Rome, 132
  Siena, 137
  Spoleto, 135
  Valle D'Aosta, 141
  Valsorda, 134
  Venice, 143
  Verona, 143
  Volterra, 137
Netherlands
  Amsterdam, 149–150
  in general, 149
  Haarlem, 150
  Hoge Veluwe, 151
  Leiden, 151
  The Hague, 151
Norway
  Aurlandsfjord and
    Flam, 161
  Bergen, 160
  Geirangerfjord, 161
  in general, 155
  Jostedalspreen Glacier,
    161
  Kristansand, 162
  Lillehammer, 159
  Oslo, 158
  Romsdalsfjord and
    Trollveggen, 162
  Stavanger, 162
Poland
  Czestochowa, 170
  Gdansk, 171
  in general, 167
  Krakow, 169
  Leba, 170
  Sopot, 170–171
  Warsaw, 168
  Zakopane, 169
  Zamosc, 170

Portugal
  Berlenga Island, 179
  Cascais, 177
  in general, 175
  Lisbon, 176
  Obidos, 180
  Oporto, 180
  Peneda-Geres, 181
  Sintra, 177
  Tavira, 178
  Viana do Castelo, 180
  Vila Vicosa, 179
registration, 28
Spain
  Baleraric Islands, 192
  Barcelona, 190
  Cordoba, 194
  Costa Brava, 191
  El Escorial, 187
  in general, 185
  Granada, 193
  Madrid, 186
  Malmo, 204
  Montserrat, 190
  Salamanca, 187
  San Sebastian, 194
  Segovia, 188
  Sevilla, 193
  Tarragonia, 190
  Toledo, 189
  Valencia, 193
Sweden
  in general, 199
  Gothenburg, 203
  Lake Siljan area, 205
  Lund, 204
  Mariefred, 201
  Stockholm, 201
  Uppsala, 202
  Vadstena, 205
  Visby Island, 205
Switzerland
  Basel, 217
  Bellinzona, 213
  Berne, 210
  Brienz, 212
  Chur, 214
  in general, 209
  Interlaken, 211
  Jungfrau Region, 211–
    212
  Locarno, 213
  Lucerne, 216
  Lugano, 213

Maloja, 214
Pontresina, 214
Stein, 215
St. Gallen, 215
Wilderswil near Inter-
  laken, 211
Zurich, 216
Western Turkey
  Ayvalik, 226
  Bodrum, 228
  Bursa, 225
  Canakkale, 226
  Ephesus, 228
  Foca, 227
  in general, 221
  Ismir, 227
  Istanbul, 224
  Pamukkale, 228
  Western Mediterra-
    nean Coast, 229
Canakkale, Western Turkey,
  225–226
Canals, Sweden, Gothenburg,
  202
Canal trips
  Denmark, Netto Badene in
    Copenhagen, 71
  Sweden
    Gota Canal in Bohus-
      lan, 203
    Paddan boat rides in
      Gothenburg, 202
Canoeing
  Denmark
    Naestved, 73
    Roskilde, 72
  Hungary, in general, 121
  Sweden
    in general, 199
    on lake at Rattvik, 204
Cascais, Portugal, 177
Castles
  Austria
    Hohensalzburg in
      Salzburg, 50
    Konopiste in Benesov,
      61
  Czech Republic
    Cesky Krumlov in
      Ceske Budejovice,
      60, 62
    Karlstejn, 60
    the Prague in Prague,
      60

Denmark
  Egeskov in Odense, 73
  Frederiksborg Slot in
    Hillerod, 72
  Kronborg Slot in Hels-
    ingor, 72
  Rosenborg Slot in
    Copenhagen, 70
Germany
  Heidelberg, 102
  King Ludwig II's in
    Garmisch-Partenkir-
    chen, 101
Hungary
  Castle Hill area in
    Budapest, 122
  Eger ruins in Eger, 127
  Keszthely in Balaton
    Lake, 124
  Szentendre, 123
Norway, Akershus in Oslo,
  157
Poland
  Pieskowa in Krakow,
    169
  Wawel in Krakow, 169
Portugal, Castelo de Sao
    Jorge in Lisbon, 176
Sweden
  Malmohus in Malmo,
    203
  Vadstena, 205
  Visby Island, 205
Switzerland
  Bellinzona, 213
  Thun, 212
Cathedrals
  Austria, St. Stephens in Vi-
    enna, 51
  France
    Cathedrale Sainte
      Marie in Bayonne,
      90
    Lourdes, 91
    Notre Dame, Paris, 81
    Sacre Coeur, Paris, 81
  Germany, Cologne, 105
  Hungary, Esztergom, 123
  Italy
    Assisi, 133
    proper attire, 132
    St. Peter's in Rome, 132
    Vatican in Rome, 132

Poland
Czestochowa, 170
Wawel in Krakow, 169
Portugal, Evora Cathedral
in Evora, 179
Spain
Catedral in Segovia,
188
Catedral Nueva in Sala-
manca, 187
Cathedral of Santa Mar-
ia de la Sede in
Sevilla, 193
Sweden
Domkyrkan in Uppsa-
la, 201
Lund, 204
Switzerland, Kloster St.
Gallen, 215
Western Turkey
Kizil Avlu (Red Basili-
ca) in Bergama, 226
St. John Basilica in
Ephesus, 227
Cauterets, France, 91
Caves
Greece, Blue Caves on Is-
land of Zakynthos,
116
Hungary, Aggtelek Nation-
al Park, 127
Italy, Valsorda, 134
Spain, Altamira with paint-
ings, 185
Western Turkey, Yereba-
tan cistern in Istan-
bul, 224
Ceske Budejovice, Czech Re-
public, 62
Cezanne, birthplace of, 88
Chair lifts
Austria, Lechtaler Alps, 53
Czech Republic, Slovakia,
63
Sweden, Mickeltemplet,
206
Chalets, Czech Republic, Slo-
vakia, 64
Chamonix, France, 86
Cheese making
Netherlands, Amsterdam,
149
Switzerland, Stein, 215

Chicken
with mushrooms and
wine, 39
with mushrooms, cream
and brandy, 38
with tomatoes and olives,
42–43
Chopin, museum, 168
Chur, Switzerland, 214
Churches
Hungary
Byzantine Votive in
Szeged, 126
Great Reformed in De-
brecen, 126
Italy
Basilica di San
Francesco in Assisi,
133
Church of San Lorenzo
in Florence, 136
Medici Chapel in Flo-
rence, 136
Norway
Mariakirken in Bergen,
160
Stavanger Domkirke,
162
Poland, Sigismund, in Kra-
kow, 169
Portugal, Madres de Deus
in Lisbon, 176
Spain, Panteon de Goya in
Madrid, 186
Clothing
Norway, 155, 161
packing, 14
Switzerland, 209
Cogwheel trains, Switzerland
Brienz, 212
Interlaken, 211
Mount Pilatus, 216
Colmar, France, 92
Cologne, Germany, 105
Concarneau, France, 94
Concentration camps, Po-
land, 169
Convents
Czech Republic, Loreta in
Prague, 60
Portugal, Cork Convent in
Sintra, 177
Cooking
cleaning up, 35

preparation, 32
techniques, 33–35
utensils, 16
Copenhagen, Denmark, 70–
71
average temperatures and
rainfall, 241
Cordoba, Spain, 194
Cortona, Italy, 137
Costa Brava, Spain, 191
Costs
camping places, 28
equipment, 4
per day, 2
reducing, 7
tent vs. camper van, 4
vehicle rental, 9–11
Cote d'Azur Area, France, 88–
89
Crete, Greece, 113–114
Cruises, Western Turkey,
Western Mediterra-
nean Coast, 229
Cuckoo clocks, Germany,
Black Forest, 103
Cuenca, Spain, 188
Curing, meats, 33–34
Czech and Slovak Republics,
58–67
Czechoslovakia, tempera-
tures and rainfall,
241
Czech Republic, Weekly Auto
Rental Rates, 240
Czestochowa, Poland, 170

D

Danube Bend Area, Hungary,
123
Danube River Area, Germany,
103
Davos, Switzerland, 214
D-Day landing beaches,
France, Normandy,
92–93
Debrecen, Hungary, 126–127
Definitions, cooking, 46
Delphi, Greece, 111–112
Denmark, 68–77
International Camper Van
Rental, 237
temperatures and rainfall,
241

Weekly Auto Rental Rates,
240
Dictionaries, foreign lan-
guage, 11
Didyma, Western Turkey, 227
Dijon, France, 85
Directions
pick up site, 12
who to ask for, 27
Discount cards
Federal International
Youth Travel Orga-
nization Card (FIY-
TO), 238
International Student Iden-
tity Card (ISIC), 238
Senior Citizen Card, 239
Documents
photocopies, 12
travel, 9, 238
Dollar, International Vehicle
Rental, 236
Dolomites and South Tyrol, It-
aly, 142–143
Dressings, salad, 40, 45–46
Driving
Austria, 49
Czech and Slovak Repub-
lics, 59
Denmark, 69
France, 79
Germany, 99
Greece, 109
Hungary, 121
International Driving Per-
mit (IDP), 238
Italy, 131
Netherlands, 149
Norway, 156
Poland, 167
Portugal, 175
Spain, 185
Sweden, 199–200
Switzerland, 210
Western Turkey, 222
See also Accidents; Roads;
Road signs

E

Eger, Hungary, 127
El Escorial, Spain, 187
Engadine Valley, Switzerland,
214–215

Ephesus, Western Turkey,
227–228
Epidaurus, Greece, 112
Equipment
comfort items, 17
costs, 4
list of necessary, 15–17
sleeping, 16
Estoril, Portugal, 177
Esztergom, Hungary, 123
Etiquette
France, language use, 80
Western Turkey, 222
Evora, Portugal, 178–179

F

Factories, Norway, sardine
canning in Sta-
vanger, 162
Farhenheit, home of, 171
Faro, Portugal, 178
Federal International Youth
Travel Organiza-
tion Card (FIYTO),
238
Ferries
Hungary, Danube Bend
Area, 123
Italy, Venice, 143
Norway
Aurlandsfjord and
Flam, 161
Geirangerfjord, 161
Portugal, Berlenga Island,
179
Sweden
Bohuslan, 203
in general, 199
Stockholm to Drott-
ningholm, 201
Visby Island, 205
Western Turkey
in general, 222
on the Bosphorus from
Istanbul, 224
Festivals
Portugal, Viana do Caste-
lo, 180
Spain, Sevilla, 193
Film festivals, Switzerland, Lo-
carno, 213
Finland
temperatures and rainfall,
241

Weekly Auto Rental Rates,
240
Fish
brushing oil, 34
town, Dragor, 71
market
Bergen, Norway, 160
Malmo, Sweden, 204
Fishing
Denmark, Jutland, 74
Switzerland, Davosersee in
Davos, 214
Florence, Italy, 136–137
Flowers
Austria, Kitzbuhel, 54
best time for spectacular, 7
Hungary, Western Tran-
danubia, 124
Netherlands, in general,
149
Sweden, Malmo's squares,
203
Switzerland
Jungfrau Region, 211
Locarno, 213
Swiss National Park, 215
timing trip for, 7–8
Foca, Western Turkey, 227
Folk museums See Open air
museums
Food markets
Austria
Innsbruck, 53
Kitzbuhel, 54
Salzburg, 50
Salzkammerg Ut
Region, 51
Vienna, 52
Czech and Slovak Repub-
lics, in general, 59–
60
Czech Republic, Brno, 63
Denmark
Copenhagen, 71
in general, 70
France
Aix en Provence, 88
Arles, 87
Avignon, 87
Bayonne, 90
Beaune, 85
Biarritz, 90
Blois, 84
Cauterets, 91

Chamonix, 87
Colmar, 92
Cote d'Azur (French
    Riveria), 89
Dijon, 85
in general, 79
Grenoble, 86
Lyon, 86
Menton, 89
Nancy, 92
Normandy, 93
Quimper, 94
Saint Malo, 94
Strasbourg, 92
Germany
Cologne, 105
Freudenstadtand in the
    Black Forest, 103
in general, 99
Munich, 100
Greece
Athens, 111
in general, 110
Hania, Crete, 114
Hungary, in general, 121
Italy
Assisi, 133
Cortona, 137
Florence, 136
Gran Sasso, 140
Marche, 139
Milan, 142
Montepulciano, 138
Pergugia, 133
Rivera di Ponente, 141
Rome, 132
Siena, 137
Spoleto, 135
Venice, 143
Netherlands, in general,
    149
Norway
Bergen, 160
in general, 156
Oslo, 158
Stavanger, 162
Torget in Bergen, 160
Poland, in general, 167
Portugal
in general, 175
Lisbon, 177
Oporto, 180
Sintra, 177
Tavira, 178

Viana do Castelo, 180
Vila Vicosa, 179
Spain
Baleraric Islands, 192
Barcelona, 190
Cordoba, 194
El Escorial, 187
in general, 185
Granada, 193
Malmo, 204
San Sebastian, 194
Segovia, 188
Sevilla, 193
Toledo, 189
Valencia, 193
Sweden
in general, 200
Gothenburg, 203
Stockholm, 201
Uppsala, 202
Switzerland
Basel, 217
Bellinzona, 213
Berne, 210
in general, 209
Locarno, 213
Lucerne, 216
St. Gallen, 215
Wilderswil near Inter-
    laken, 211
Zurich, 216
using, 233
Western Turkey
Ayvalik, 227
Bodrum, 228
Bursa, 225
in general, 221
Istanbul, 224
Western Mediterra-
    nean Coast, 229
Foremost Euro-Car, Interna-
    tional Vehicle Rent-
    al, 236
Forests, Poland, Pomerania,
    170
Forms, direction fill-in, 5
Fortresses, Spain, Alcazar in
    Segovia, 188
France, 78–96
temperatures and rainfall,
    241
Weekly Auto Rental Rates,
    240
Frankfurt, Germany, 104

average temperatures and
    rainfall, 241
French Alps Area, France, 86–
    87
French Riviera, France, 88–89
Fuel, costs, 10
Funen, Denmark, 73
Furado Grande, Berlenga Is-
    land, 179

G

Galleries, Italy, Galleria
    dell'Accademia in
    Venice, 143
Gallipoli, Western Turkey at
    Canakkale, 225
Gardens
Austria
    Alpenblumengarten in
        Kitzbuhel, 54
    Helbrunn in Salzburg,
        50
    Mirabell in Salzburg, 50
France
    Alsace-Lorraine area,
        91–92
    Luxembourg in Paris,
        81
    Monet's in Giverny, 82
Germany, Frankfurt, 104
Italy, Cogne Valley, 141
Netherlands
    Hoge Veluwe, 151
    Keukenhof in Haarlem,
        150
    Leiden's botanical, 151
Portugal, Monserrate in
    Colares, 177
Sweden
    Linne Garden in Uppsa-
        la, 201
    Visby Island, 205
Switzerland
    Bellinzona, Piora Al-
        pine, 213
    Interlaken, 211
Garmisch-Partenkirchen, Ger-
    many, 101
Gascogne Area, France, 91
Gasoline, purchasing, 234
Gay Capital, Greece, Island of
    Mykonos, 116
Gdansk, Poland, 171
Geirangerfjord, Norway, 161

Genoa, Italy, 140
Germany, 98–107
 temperatures and rainfall, 241–242
 Weekly Auto Rental Rates, 240
Giverny, France, 82
Glaciers
 Norway, Jostedalspreen, 161
 Switzerland, Jungfrau Region, 211
Gothenburg, Sweden, 202–203
Granada, Spain, 193–194
Gran Sasso, Italy, 139–140
Graubunden, Switzerland, 214
Great Plain Puszta, Hungary, 126–127
Greece, 108–119
 cost per day, 2–3
 historical sights, 7
 International Camper Van Rental, 237
 temperatures and rainfall, 242
 Weekly Auto Rental Rates, 240
Grenoble, France, 86
Grieg, Edvard, home of, 160
Groceries
 basic supplies, 30
 shopping for, 29
Gubbio, Italy, 134

H

Haarlem, Netherlands, 150
Hague, Netherlands, 151
Hallstatt, Austria, 51
Hania, Crete, Greece, 114
Harbors
 Norway, Bergen, 160
 See also Ports
Haydn, home of, 51
Heidelberg, Germany, 102
Helsingor, Denmark, 72
Helsinki, Finland, average temperatures and rainfall, 241
Herculaneum, Italy, 140
Hertz
 International Camper Van Rental, 237

International Vehicle Rental, 236
Hevelius, home of, 171
Hiking
 Austria
  Innsbruck, 52
  Lechtaler Alps, 53
  Leinz, 54
  Salzburger Sportwelt Amade, 51
  Salzkammerg Ut Region, 51
  Zell am Zeller, 54
 Czech Republic, Slovakia, 64
 France
  Basque country, 90
  Cauterets, 91
  French Alps, 86
 Germany
  Bavarian Forest (Bayerischer Wald), 102
  in general, 99
 Greece, Samaria Gorge on Crete, 114
 Hungary, Pecs, 125
 Italy
  Dolomites and South Tyrol, 142–143
  Gran Sasso, 139
  Valle D'Aosta, 141–142
 Poland, Zakopane, 168
 Portugal, Northern Spanish Border, 181
 Spain
  Baleraric Islands, 192
  Costa Brava, 191
 Sweden
  in general, 199
  Mickeltemplet, 206
 Switzerland
  Appenzell, 215
  Central Switzerland, 216
  Engadine Valley, 214
  in general, 209–210
  Interlaken, 211
  Jungfrau Region, 211
  Locarno, 213
  Maloja, 214
  Mount Pilatus and Rigi Kulm, 216
  Pontresina, 214
Hillerod, Denmark, 72

Hippocrates, birthplace, 115
Hoge Veluwe, Netherlands, 151
Horseback riding, Norway, Lillehammer, 159
Horse shows
 Austria, Vienna, 52
 Hungary, Bugac, 126
Hungary, 120–129
 Northern, 127
 temperatures and rainfall, 242
 Weekly Auto Rental Rates, 240

I

Ice caves
 Austria, Hallstatt, 51
 Switzerland, Jungfrau Region, 211
Identification
 International Camping Carnet Card, 239
 International Student Identity Card (ISIC), 238
Innsbruck, Austria, 52–53
Insurance, vehicle, 11, 235
Interlaken, Switzerland, 211
International
 Camping Carnet Card, 239
 Driving Permit (IDP), 238
 Student Identity Card (ISIC), 238
Iraklion, Crete, Greece, 113
Ireland, temperatures and rainfall, 242
Island of
 Corfu, Greece, 115
 Folegandros, Greece, 117
 Kos, Greece, 115
 Mykonos, Greece, 116
 Naoussa, Greece, 116
 Paros, Greece, 116–117
 Patmos, Greece, 115
 Rhodes, Greece, 114
 Samothrace, Greece, 115
 Skiathos, Greece, 116
 Thira (Santorini), Greece, 117
 Tilos, Greece, 114
 Zakynthos, Greece, 116
Ismir, Turkey, 227
Istanbul, Western Turkey, 223–224

Italy, 130–146
  historical sights, 7
  International Camper Van
    Rental, 237
  Northern, 140–141
  temperatures and rainfall,
    242
  Weekly Auto Rental Rates,
    240
Itinerary, planning your, 7–8

J

Julienne, defined, 46
Jungfrau Region, Switzerland,
  211–212
Jutland, Denmark, 74–75

K

Kale, onion and potato saute
  or soup, 40
Karlovy Vary, Czech Repub-
  lic, 61
Kayaking
  Italy, Valle D'Aosta, 141–
    142
  Switzerland
    Interlaken, 211
    Lucerne, 216
Kecskemet, Hungary, 126
Kemwel, International Vehi-
  cle Rental, 236
Keszthely, Hungary, 125
Kitzbuhel, Austria, 54
Knossos, Crete, Greece, 113
Kodaly, Zoltan, birthplace,
  126
Krakow, Poland, 169
Kristansand, Norway, 162
Kutna Hora, Czech Republic,
  61

L

Lace, Sweden, Vadstena, 206
Lago Trasimeno, Italy, 134
Lake Region, Switzerland, 212
Lakes
  Germany
    Bavarian Alps, 101
    Lake Constance (Bod-
      ensee), 103
    Mummelsee in the
      Black Forest, 103
  Hungary
    Balaton, 124

Lake Gyogy, 125
Italy
  Lago di Como, 144
  Lago di Garda, 143
  Lago di Maggiore, 144
  Lago Trasimeno, 134
Poland, Lebsko Lake in Le-
  ba, 170
Sweden
  Lake Siljan area, 204–
    205
  Lake Vanern in Bohus-
    lan, 203
Switzerland
  Interlaken, 211
  Locarno, 213
  Lugano, 213
  Rhitom, 213
  Thun, 212
Language, direction fill-in
  forms, 5
Leba, Poland, 170
Lechtaler Alps, Austria, 53
Leiden, Netherlands, 151
Leinz, Austria, 54
Lillehammer, Norway, 159
Lisbon, Portugal, 176–177
  average temperatures and
    rainfall, 243
Liszt, museum, 124
Locarno, Switzerland, 213
Loire Valley, France, 83–84
Lourdes, France, 91
Lucca, Italy, 138
Lucerne, Switzerland, 216
Lugano, Switzerland, 213
Luggage, what you'll need, 4
Lund, Sweden, 204
Lyon, France, 85–86

M

Madrid, Spain, 186
  average temperatures and
    rainfall, 241
Madurodam, Netherlands,
  151
Malls, Denmark, Stroget in
  Copenhagen, 70
Malmo, Sweden, 203–204
Maloja, Switzerland, 214
Maps
  Austria, 48
  Czech and Slovak Repub-
    lics, 58

Denmark, 68, 70
France, 78
Germany, 98
Greece, 109
Hungary, 120–21
Italy, 130
Netherlands, 148
Norway, 154
Poland, 166
Portugal, 174
purchasing, 11
resources, 239
Spain, 184
Sweden, 198
Switzerland, 208
using your, 12
Western Turkey, 220
Marche, Italy, 138–139
Margaret Island, Hungary, 122
Marianske Lazne, Czech Re-
  public, 62
Marinating, meats, 33
Meats
  cooking, 32–33
  marination oil, 34
Metro
  Barcelona, 189
  Madrid, 187
  Paris, 81–82
Milan, Italy, 141–142
Mileage, a day's journey, 8
Miletus, Western Turkey, 227
Mines
  Czech Republic, Kutna
    Hora, 61
  Poland, Wieliczka, 169
  Sweden, Koppargruva in
    Lake Siljan area,
    204
Minorca, Baleraric Islands,
  Spain, 192
Monasteries
  Poland, Jasna Gora in Cze-
    stochowa, 170
  Portugal
    Jeronimos in Lisbon,
      176
    Santa Maria in Alcoba-
      ca, 179
  Spain, Montserrat, 190
  See also Abbeys
Monet, home and gardens, 82
Monsaraz, Portugal, 179
Montalcino, Italy, 138

Montepulciano, Italy, 138
Montmarte, Paris, 81
Montserrat, Spain, 190
Mont St.-Michel, France, 93
Moped riding, Spain, Balerar-
    ic Islands, 192
Moravia, Czech and Slovak
    Republics, 63
Mosques
    Spain, Mezquita in Cordo-
        ba, 194
    Western Turkey
        Beyazit Camii in Bursa,
            225
        Blue Mosque in Istan-
            bul, 224
        Suleymaniye in Istan-
            bul, 224
        Yesil Camii (Green
            Mosque) in Bursa,
            225
Moulin Rouge, Paris, 81
Mountain climbing, Norway,
    Romsdalsfjord and
    Trollveggen, 162
Mountaineering Schools,
    Switzerland, Pontre-
    sina, 214
Mount Pilatus, Switzerland,
    216
Mozart, home of, 51
Mt. Vesuvius, Italy, 140
Munich, Germany, 100
    average temperatures and
        rainfall, 242
Museums
    Austria
        Helbrunn Folklore in
            Salzburg, 50
        Kunsthistorisches Mu-
            seum in Vienna, 52
    Czech Republic
        Beer Brewing in Plzen,
            62
        Hradek in Kutna Hora,
            61
        Slovak National Upris-
            ing in Banska Bystri-
            ca, 60
        State Jewish in Prague,
            60
        Tatra National Park in
            Tatranska Lomni-
            ca, 60, 63

        Technological in Brno,
            60, 63
    Denmark
        Copenhagen's small,
            71
        Frilandsmuseet in Lyn-
            gby, 71
        Hans Christian Anders-
            en in Odense, 73
        Jernbanemuseet in
            Odense, 73
        Louisiana Museum of
            Modern Art in Hum-
            lebaek, 71
        Mosegard Prehistoric
            in Arhus, 74
        Nationalmuseet in
            Copenhagen, 70
        Ny Carlsberg in Copen-
            hagen, 70
        Vikingeskibshallen in
            Roskilde, 72
    France
        Burgundy and Rhone
            Valley, 85–86
        Center Georges Pompi-
            dou in Paris, 81
        Louvre in Paris, 81
        Lyon, 85
        Musee de l'Orangerie
            in Paris, 81
        Musee d'Orsay in Paris,
            81
        Musee Picasso in Paris,
            81
        Rodin in Paris, 81
    Germany
        Deutsch in Munich, 100
        Frankfurt, 104
        Mercedes Benz in Stut-
            tgart, 102
        Pinakothck in Munich,
            100
        Porsche in Stuttgart,
            102
    Greece
        Archaeological in Irak-
            lion, Crete, 113
        Delphi, 111
        in general, 109
        Island of Thira (Santori-
            ni), 117

    National Archaeologi-
        cal Museum in Ath-
        ens, 110
Hungary
    archaeological in Pecs,
        125
    Deri in Debrecen, 126
    Eger Castle in Eger, 127
    Fine Arts in Budapest,
        122
    hours, 121
    Liszt Ferenc in Sopron,
        124
    National Museum in
        Budapest, 122
    Wine museum in
        Tokaj, 127
Italy
    Florence, 136
    National museum in
        Florence, 136
    Rome, 132
    The Accademia in Flo-
        rence, 136
    Uffizi Gallery in Flo-
        rence, 136
Netherlands
    Amsterdam, 149
    Kroller-Muller in Hoge
        Veluwe, 151
Norway
    Bryggen in Bergen, 160
    Fram in Oslo, 157
    Hanseatic in Bergen,
        160
    Historic Vehicle in
        Lillehammer, 159
    Holmenkollen Ski
        Jump in Oslo, 157
    Kon-Tiki in Oslo, 157
    Maihaugen Folk in
        Lillehammer, 159
    Munch in Oslo, 157
    Norwegian Folk in Os-
        lo, 157
    Viking Ship in Oslo, 157
Poland
    Chopin in Zelazowa
        Wola (near War-
        saw), 168
    Czartoryski Art in Kra-
        kow, 169
    National in Warsaw,
        168

Portugal
in general, 175
Gulbenkian Museum in
Lisbon, 176
Museu de Arts Decora-
tiva in Lisbon, 176
Museu de Evora in Evo-
ra, 179
Museu de Marinha in
Lisbon, 176
Museu dos Azulejos in
Lisbon, 176
Museu dos Coches in
Lisbon, 176
Praca da Republica in
Sintra, 177
Spain
Alcazar in Toledo, 189
Archaeological Muse-
um in Madrid, 186
Archivo de las Indias in
Sevilla, 193
Cadaques on the Costa
Brava, 191
Cason del Buen Retiro
in Madrid, 186
El Prado in Madrid, 186
Inglesia de San Tome
in Toledo, 189
Miro in Barcelona, 189
Museo de Ceramica in
Valencia, 192
Museo de la Santa Cruz
in Toledo, 189
Picasso in Barcelona,
189
Sweden
Gammelgards in Lake
Siljan area, 204
Kanalmuseum in Bo-
huslan, 203
Koppargruva in Lake
Siljan area, 204
Linne Museum in Upp-
sala, 201
Maritima Centrum in
Gothenburg, 202
mideval museum in
Lund, 204
Skansen (Vasa ship
museum) in Stock-
holm, 200
Vasamuseet in Stock-
holm, 201

Switzerland
Am Romerholz Oskar Re-
inhart, Winterthur,
216
Basel, 217
Berne, 210
Davos Kirchner Muse-
um in Daovs, 214
Kunsthaus in Zurich,
215
Picasso in Lucerne, 216
Richard Wagner in Luc-
erne, 216
Schweizerische
Landesmuseum in
Zurich, 215
Transport in Lucerne,
216
Western Turkey
Archaeology Museum
in Bergama, 226
Ayasofya in Istanbul,
223
Ephesus, 227
Ethnology Museum in
Ismir, 227
Museum of Archaeolo-
gy in Bodrum, 228
Naval Museum in
Canakkale, 226
Turkish and Islamic
Arts Museum in
Istanbul, 224
Mushroom, onion and potato
saute or soup, 40
Music. See Performances, mu-
sical
Mycenae, Greece, 112
Mystra, Greece, 112

N

Nancy, France, 92
Napoleon Bonaparte, 63
National parks
Austria, Hohe Tauern in
Zell am Zeller, 54
Czech Republic, Tatra in
Vratna Valley, 63
France, Parc National des
Pyrenees Near Cau-
terets, 91
Greece, Samaria Gorge on
Crete, 114

Hungary
Aggtelek, 127
Hortobagy in Debre-
cen, 127
Kiskunsay in Bugac,
126
Italy
Abruzzo, 140
Gran Paradiso in Valle
D'Aosta, 141
Netherlands, Hoge Velu-
we, 151
Poland, Slowinski in Leba,
170
Portugal, Peneda-Geres,
181
Spain, Costa Brava, 191
Switzerland, Swiss Nation-
al Park, 215
National parks, See also Parks
Navigator, duties, 22–23
Nazare, Portugal, 179
Netherlands, 148–153
flowers, 7
International Camper Van
Rental, 237
temperatures and rainfall,
243
Weekly Auto Rental Rates,
240
Nice, France, average temper-
atures and rainfall,
241
Normandy Area, France, 92–
93
Norway, 154–164
International Camper Van
Rental, 237
temperatures and rainfall,
243
Weekly Auto Rental Rates,
240
Nuremberg, Germany, 100

O

Obidos, Portugal, 180
Odense, Denmark, 73
Old towns
Czech Republic
Cesky Krumlov, 62
Plzen, 62
Prague, 60

Denmark
    Den Fynske Landsby, 73
    Den Gamle By in Arhus, 74
    Dragor on Amager island, 71
    Ribe, 74
    Tonder, 75
France
    Aix en Provence, 88
    Avignon, 87
    Beaune, 85
    Dijon, 85
    Ile de la Cite, 81
    Lyon, 85
    Nancy, 92
    St. John-de-Pied-de-Port, 90
    Strasbourg, 91
    Vittel, 92
Germany
    in general, 99
    Nuremberg, 100
Greece
    Corfu, 115
    Hania, 114
    Lindos, 114
    Mykonos, 116
Hungary
    Budapest, 122
    Sopron, 124
Italy
    Tuscany, 136–138
Norway
    Fredrikstak near Oslo, 157
    Gamle Stavanger in Stavanger, 162
Poland
    Chocholow near Zakopane, 169
    Warsaw, 168
    Zakopane, 168
    Zamosc, 170
Portugal, Tavira, 178
Spain
    Bari Gotic in Barcelona, 189
    Castell de Morella in Valencia, 192
    Cuenca, 188
    Segovia, 188
    Toledo, 189

Sweden
    Gamala Stan in Stockholm, 200
    Mariefred, 201
    Mariestad, 203
Switzerland
    Berne, 210
    Corippo, 213
    Lavertezzo, 213
    Lucerne, 216
    St. Gallen, 215
    Thun, 212
    Wilderswil near Interlaken, 211
Western Turkey, Cumali Kizik near Bursa, 225
Olive oil, Western Turkey, Ayvalik, 226
Olympia, Grece, 112
Open air museums
    Denmark
        Arhus, 74
        Lejre, 72
        Ribe, 74
    Norway
        Lillehammer, 159
        Oslo, 157
    Sweden
        Lake Siljan Area, 204
        Stockholm, 200
Open markets. See Food markets
Opera houses
    France, Opera Garnier in Paris, 81
    Italy, La Scala opera house in Milan, 142
    Spain, Gran Theatre del Liceu in Barcelona, 189
Oporto, Portugal, 180
Orangery, Austria, Mirabell in Salzburg, 50
Orivieto, Italy, 135
Orleans, France, 83
Oslo, Norway, 157
    average temperatures and rainfall, 243

P

Packing
    baggage, 12–15
    comfort items, 17–18

personal items, 18
Paddle steamer, Norway, Lillehammer, 159
Palaces
    Austria
        Helbrunn in Salzburg, 50
        Imperial, Vienna, 51
        Mirabell in Salzburg, 50
        Schonbrunn in Vienna, 51
    Czech Republic, Hluboka nad Vltavou in Ceske Budejovice, 62
    France, Palais des Papes in Avignon, 87
    Germany, Residenz in Munich, 100
    Greece, Knossos on Crete, 113
    Hungary
        Esterhazy in Sopron, 124
        Festetics in Keszthely, 125
        Royal in Budapest, 122
        Varmuzeum in Esztergom, 123
    Italy
        Bargello in Florence, 136
        Genoa, 140
        Palazzo Ducale in Venice, 143
        Pitti in Florence, 136
    Poland
        Lazienki in Warsaw, 167
        Royal Palace in Warsaw, 167
        Wilanow in Warsaw, 167
    Portugal
        Paco Ducal in Vila Vicosa, 179
        Palacio de Pena in Sintra, 177
        Palacio Nacional de Sintra in Sintra, 177
    Spain, Palacio de Marques in Valencia, 192

Sweden, Drottningholm
near Stockholm,
201
Western Turkey
Dolmabahce in Istan-
bul, 224
Topkapi in Istanbul,
223
Yidiz in Istanbul, 224
Pamukkale, Western Turkey,
228
Paragliding
Switzerland
Interlaken, 211
Lucerne, 216
Paris, France, 81–82
average temperatures and
rainfall, 241
Parking
Denmark, 69
general rules for, 234
Norway, Oslo, 158
Spain, 185
Parks
Germany, Englischer Gar-
ten in Munich, 100
Hungary, Nagyerdo Forest
in Debrecen, 127
Italy, Genoa, 140
Norway, Vigeland Sculp-
tural in Oslo, 157
Poland, Lazienki in War-
saw, 167
Spain
Ciudad Encantada in
Cuenca, 188
Parc Guell in Barcelo-
na, 189
Sweden
Djurgarden in Stock-
holm, 200
Spaceport Liseberg
amusement park in
Gothenburg, 202
Switzerland, Piora Alpine
Park near Airolo,
213
Western Turkey, Yidiz in
Istanbul, 224
See also National Parks
Passport, 238
Pasta
with cherry tomatoes, gar-
lic and basil, 41

cooking, 34
with eggplant, garlic and
basil, 41
with tomatoes, garlic and
basil, 41–42
Tuscan meat sauce, 44
Pecs, Hungary, 125
Peloponnese, Greece 111
Performances, ballet
Czech Republic, Brno, 63
Italy, Verona, 143
Performances, musical
Austria
Leinz, 54
Salzburg, 50
Vienna, 51
Zell am Zeller, 54
Denmark
Arhus, 74
Copenhagen, 71
Romo, 75
Hungary, in general, 121
Poland
Krakow, 169
Poland, Sopot, 170
Warsaw, 167
Portugal
Fado in Lisbon, 176
Viana do Castelo, 180
Spain, Costa Brava, 191
Switzerland
Berne, 210
Davos, 214
Performances, opera
Czech Republic
Bratislava, 65
Brno, 63
Italy, Verona, 143
Pergugia, Italy, 133
Phaestos, Crete, Greece, 113
Pharmacies, Western Turkey,
223
Photocopies
"Asking for Directions"
forms, 14
documents, 12
Phrases, common French, 80
Picasso, home of, 87
Pick up site, directions, 12
Piza, Italy, 138
Plzen, Czech Republic, 62
Poland, 166–173
International Camper Van
Rental, 237

temperatures and rainfall,
243
Weekly Auto Rental Rates,
240
Polenta, cooking, 35
Pomerania, Poland, 170–171
Pompeii, Italy, 140
Pontresina, Switzerland, 214
Pork
curing, 33–34
Ports
France
Concarneau, 94
Rue du Port Neuf in
Bayonne, 90
Greece, Hania, Crete, 114
Norway
Kristansand, 162
Stavanger, 162
Poland, Gdansk, 171
Sweden, Gothenburg, 202
Western Turkey
Foca, 227
Ismir, 227
See also Harbors
Portugal, 174–183
International Camper Van
Rental, 237
temperatures and rainfall,
243
Weekly Auto Rental Rates,
240
Potatoes, with broccoli and
onions, 38
Prague, Cezehoslovakia, 60–
61
average temperatures and
rainfall, 241
Priene, Western Turkey, 227
Provence Area, France, 87
Public transit
Denmark, Copenhagen, 71
France, Paris, 81–82
Greece, Crete, 114
Norway, Oslo, 158
Portugal, Lisbon, 176
Spain
Barcelona, 189
Madrid, 187
Sweden
Gothenburg, 203
Stockholm, 201

Switzerland, in general,
    209
  using, 233

Q

Quimper, France, 93–94

R

Radhus, Sweden, Vadstena,
    206
Rafting
  Czech Republic, Slovakia,
    64
  Italy, Valle D'Aosta, 141–
    142
  Switzerland, Interlaken,
    211
Railways
  Hungary, Cog railway in
    Budapest, 122
  Norway, Aurlandsfjord
    and Flam, 161
  Switzerland
    cogwheel
      Brienz, 212
      Mount Pilatus, 216
      Wilderswil, 211
    narrow gauge in Ap-
      penzell, 215
Rainfall, average, 241–244
Recipes, camping, 37–46
Renting, vehicles, 9–11, 236
Reservations
  airfares, 8–9
  vehicle, 11
Resorts
  Poland, Sopot, 170
  Switzerland, Graubunden
    area, 214
Restaurants
  Austria, 50
  Denmark, 70
  France, 80
  Germany, 99
  Greece, 110
  Italy, 131
  Norway, 156
  Spain, 186
  Sweden, 200
  Western Turkey, 223
Rhineland Area, Germany,
    104–105
Rhone Valley Area, France,
    85–86

Ribe, Denmark, 74
Rice, with apples, nuts and
    raisins, 39–40
Rigi Kulm, Switzerland, 216
Rivera di Ponente, Italy, 141
Rivers
  Germany, Danube, 103
  Hungary, Danube, 122
Roads, Austria, Grossglockner
    Strasse at Zell am
    Zeller, 54
Road signs
  Germany, 99
  Greece, 109
  Hungary, 121
  International, 23–25
  Italy, in general, 131
  navigation, 22
  reading, 234
  Sweden, 200
  Western Turkey, 222
Roman baths, Western Tur-
    key, Pamukkale,
    228
Rome, Italy, 132
  average temperatures and
    rainfall, 242
Romo, Denmark, 75
Romsdalsfjord, Norway, 162
Roskilde, Denmark, 72–73
Rowing, Norway, Lilleham-
    mer, 159
Ruins
  Eger Castle in Eger, 127
  France, Arles, 87
  Greece
    Athens, 110
    Lindos on Island of
      Rhodes, 114
    Mystra, 112
    Olympia, 112
    Phaestos, Crete, 113
  Hungary, Visegrad, 123
  Italy
    Etruscan in Umbria,
      133
    Pompeii, Herculaneum
      and Mt. Vesuvius,
      140
  Spain, Castell de Morella
    in Valencia, 192
  Western Turkey
    Acropolis in Bergama,
      226

Ephesus, 227
Hellinistic in Bergama,
    226
Sardis near Ismir, 227
Truva in Canakkale,
    226
Western Mediterra-
    nean Coast, 229

S

Sacred cities, France, Lour-
    des, 91
Sailing
  Austria, Salzkammerg Ut
    Region, 51
  Switzerland, Lugano, 213
Saint Malo, France, 94
Salad
  dressings, 40, 45–46
  Provencal vegetable, 44–
    45
Salamanca, Spain, 187
Salt mines
  Germany, Garmisch-
    Partenkirchen, 101
  Hallstatt, Austria, 51
  Poland, Wieliczka near
    Krakow, 169
Salzburg, Austria, 50
Salzburger Sportwelt Amade,
    Austria, 51
Salzkammerg Ut Region, Aus-
    tria, 51
Sanctuary of the Great Gods,
    Island of Samo-
    thrace, Greece, 115
Sand dunes, Poland, Leba,
    170
San Sebastian, Spain, 194
Sauce, Tuscan meat for spa-
    ghetti, 44
Saunas, Germany, Garmisch-
    Partenkirchen, 101
Sausages, with beer and pota-
    toes, 42
Saute
  defined, 46
  mushroom, onion and po-
    tato, 40
Scheduling
  Austria, 49
  Czech and Slovak Repub-
    lics, 59
  Denmark, 69

France, 79
  Cote d'Azur, 88
Germany, 99
Greece, 109
Italy, 131
  Marche, 138
Netherlands, 149
Norway, 155
Portugal, 175
Spain, 185
for special experiences, 7–8
Sweden, 199
Switzerland, 209
Western Turkey, 221
Schopenhauer, home of, 171
Schubert, home of, 51
Security, avoiding burglary, 5
Segovia, Spain, 188
Senior Citizen Card, 239
Sevilla, Spain, 193
Shop hours
  Austria, 50
  Czech and Slovak Republics, 60
  Denmark, Copenhagen, 71
  France, 80
  Germany, 99
  Hungary, 121
  Italy, 131
  Netherlands, 149
  Norway, 156
  Portugal, 175
  Spain, 186
  Switzerland, 210
  Western Turkey, 222
Showers
  Greece, 109
  makeshift, 17
  Western Turkey, in general, 221
Siena, Italy, 137
Silk, Western Turkey, Koza Han near Bursa, 225
Sintra, Portugal, 177
Siofok, Hungary, 124
Skiing
  Austria
    Innsbruck, 52
    Salzburger Sportwelt Amade, 51
  France, Basque country, 90

Italy
  Dolomites and South Tyrol, 142–143
  Valle D'Aosta, 141–142
Poland, Zakopane, 168
Switzerland, Davos, 214
Slavkov U Brna, Czech Republic, 63
Slovak, and Czech Republics, 58–67
Slovakia, Czech and Slovak Republics, 63–65
Soap, Western Turkey, Ayvalik, 226
Soccer
  Portugal, 175-176
  Spain, Madrid, 186
Solidarity Movement, home of Poland's, 171
Sopot, Poland, 170–171
Sopron, Hungary, 124
Soup, mushroom, onion and potato, 40
Southern Transdanubia, Hungary, 125
Spain, 184–196
  International Camper Van Rental, 237
  temperatures and rainfall, 243
  Weekly Auto Rental Rates, 240
Spanish Riding School, Vienna, Austria, 52
Spa towns
  Czech Republic
    Karlovy Vary, 61
    Marianske Lazne, 62
  Germany, Baden-Baden, 102
  Hungary, Balatonfured, 125
Spoleto, Italy, 135
Springs
  Greece, Castella in Delphi, 111
  Italy, Montalcino, 138
Squares
  Italy, San Marco Piazza in Venice, 143
  Portugal, Renaissance Square in Viana do Castelo, 180

Spain, Plaza Mayor in Salamanica, 187
Sweden
  Lilla Torget in Malmo, 203
  Lund, 204
  Stortorget in Malmo, 203
  See also Malls
Stavanger, Norway, 162
Steam baths, Germany, Garmisch-Partenkirchen, 101
Stein, Switzerland, 215
Stew
  Provencal vegetable, 44–45
  Tuscan beef, 43
St. Francis of Assisi, home of, 133
St. Gallen, Switzerland, 215
Stockholm, Sweden, 200–201
  average temperatures and rainfall, 241
Storage, bicycle shipping boxes, 20
Stove
  board, 15
  packing, 15
Strasbourg, France, 91
Strauss, home of, 51
Structures
  France, Eiffel Tower in Paris, 81
  Italy
    Bridge of Sighs in Venice, 143
    Roman arena in Verona, 143
  Spain
    Alhambra in Granada, 193
    Girald tower in Sevilla, 193
    Sagrada Familia in Barcelona, 189
  Western Turkey
    Acropolis in Bergama, 226
    Galata tower and bridge in Istanbul, 224
Stuttgart, Germany, 102

Sulfur springs, Italy, Montalcino, 138
Surfing
France, Biarritz, 90
Spain, Zarautz near San Sabastian, 194
Sweden, 198–207
temperatures and rainfall, 243
Swimming
Switzerland
Davosersee in Davos, 214
Locarno, 213
Western Turkey, Western Mediterranean Coast, 229
Swiss Jura, Switzerland, 217
Switzerland, 208–219
temperatures and rainfall, 243
Weekly Auto Rental Rates, 240
Szeged, Hungary, 126
Szentendre, Hungary, 123

T

Tapes, foreign language, 11
Tarragonia, Spain, 190
Taverns, *See* Beer halls
Tavira, Portugal, 178
Temperatures, average, 241–244
Tent
packing, 13
setting up camp, 31
Textile manufacturing, Switzerland, Bodensee area, 215
The Algarve, Portugal, 178
The Hague, Netherlands, 151
Thermal waters
Czech Republic
Karlovy Vary, 61
Marianske Lazne, 62
Hungary
Balatonfured, 125
Budapest, 122
Eger, 127
in general, 121
Lake Gyogy in Keszthely, 125
Visegrad, 123
Italy, Umbria, 133

Western Turkey
Bursa, 225
Cotton Castle in Pamukkale, 228
The Sound of Music, Salzburg, Austria, 50
Thun, Switzerland, 212
Ticino, Switzerland, 212–213
Tickets, airlines, 8–9
Tihany, Hungary, 125
Tipping. *See* Restaurants
Toast, defined, 46
Tokaj, Hungary, 127
Toledo, Spain, 189
Tombs, Western Turkey, Yesil Turbe in Bursa, 225
Tourist offices
Austria
in general, 49
Innsbruck, 53
Vienna, 52
Czech and Slovak Republics, in general, 59
Czech Republic
Bratislava, 65
Prague, 61
Denmark, 70
Arhus, 74
Copenhagen, 71
in general, 70
Helsingor, 72
Odense, 73
Ribe, 74
France, 79
Aix en Provence, 88
Arles, 87
Avignon, 87
Bayeux, 93
Bayonne, 90
Beaune, 85
Biarritz, 90
Blois, 84
Bordeaux, 89
Cauterets, 91
Chamonix, 86
Colmar, 92
Concarneau, 94
Cote d'Azur (French Riviera), 89
Dijon, 85
Grenoble, 86
Lyon, 85
Menton, 89
Mont St.-Michel, 93

Nancy, 92
Nice, 89
Normandy area, 93
Orleans, 83
Quimper, 94
Saint Malo, 94
Strasbourg, 92
Germany
Cologne, 105
Frankfurt, 104
Garmisch-Partenkirchen, 101
in general, 99
Munich, 100
Rhineland, 104
Stuttgart, 102
Greece
Athens, 111
in general, 109
Island of Rhodes, 114
Olympia, 112
Italy
Florence, 136
in general, 131
Gran Paradiso National Park, 141
Gran Sasso, 140
Gubbio, 134
Perugia, 133
Piza, 138
Siena, 137
Spoleto, 135
Valle D'Aosta, 141
Netherlands
Amsterdam, 150
in general, 149
Haarlem, 150
Leiden, 151
The Hague, 151
Norway
Bergen, 160
Geirangerfjord, 161
in genreal, 156
Oslo, 157–158
Stavanger, 162
Poland
Czestochowa, 170
Gdansk, 171
in general, 167
Krakow, 169
Sopot, 170
Warsaw, 168
Zakopane, 169
Zamosc, 170

Portugal
Faro, 178
in general, 175
Lisbon, 176
Oporto, 180
Peneda-Geres, 181
Sintra, 177
Vila Vicosa, 179
Spain
Baleraric Islands, 192
Barcelona, 190
Cordoba, 194
Costa Brava, 191
El Escorial, 187
in general, 186
Granada, 193
Madrid, 186–187
Malmo, 204
Salamanca, 187
San Sebastian, 194
Segovia, 188
Sevilla, 193
Tarragonia, 190
Toledo, 189
Uppsala, 201
Valencia, 193
Sweden
in general, 200
Gothenburg, 203
Lake Siljan area, 205
Lund, 204
Stockholm, 201
Uppsala, 201
Vadstena, 204
Visby Island, 205
Switzerland
Basel, 217
Bellinzona, 213
Brienz, 212
in general, 209
Jungfrau Region, 212
Locarno, 213
Lucerne, 216
Lugano, 213
St. Gallen, 215
Wilderswil near Inter-
laken, 211
Zurich, 216
using, 233
Western Turkey
Ayvalik, 226
Bodrum, 228
Bursa, 225
Canakkale, 226

Ephesus, 227
in general, 221
Ismir, 227
Istanbul, 224
Pamukkale, 228
Western Mediterra-
nean Coast, 229
Trains *See* Railway
Travel guides, purchasing, 11
Trollveggen, Norway, 162
Troy, Western Turkey at
Canakkale, 225
Turkey
cost per day, 2–3
International Camper Van
Rental, 237
Weekly Auto Rental Rates,
240
Western, 220–231
Turkish baths
Hungary, Eger, 127
Western Turkey, 222–223
Tuscany, Italy, 136–138

U

Umbria, Italy, 133–135
Underground corridors,
Czech Republic,
Plzen, 62
Universities, Spain, Univer-
sidad in Salamanca,
187
Uppsala, Sweden, 201–202
Utensils, cooking, 16–17

V

Vadstena, Sweden, 205
Valencia, Spain, 192–193
Valle D'Aosta, Italy, 141–142
Valsorda, Italy, 134
Val Verzasca, Switzerland,
213
VAT (value added tax), 11
Vegetables, cooking, 34
Vehicle
burglary, 235
insurance, 11, 235–236
International Camper Van
Rental Companies,
237
International Car Rental
Companies, 236
pick up, 19–21
renting, 9–11, 236

Weekly Auto Rental Rates,
240
Venice, Italy, 143
average temperatures and
rainfall, 242
Verona, Italy, 143
Viana do Castelo, Portugal,
180
Vienna, Austria, 51–52
average temperatures and
rainfall, 241
Vila Vicosa, Portugal, 179
Villas, Norway, Ole Bull's in
Bergen, 160
Vinaigrette
cheese, 46
citrus, 40
herb, 46
lemon, 45
mustard, 45
Vineyards
France
Beaune, 85
Burgundy and Rhone
Valley Area, 85
Normandy, 92
Germany, Rhineland, 104–
105
Hungary
Balaton Lake, 124
Kecskemet, 126
Northern Hungary, 127
Italy, Tuscany, 136
Portugal, Oporto, 180
Visas, 238
Visby Island, Sweden, 205
Visegrad, Hungary, 123
Visitor centers
Denmark, Historical Ar-
chaeological Exper-
imental Center in
Lejre, 72
Norway, Olympic Experi-
ence in Lilleham-
mer, 159
Switzerland, Technorama
dere Schweiz in
Winterthur, 216
Western Turkey, ANZAC in
Canakkale, 225
Volcanoes
Greece, Island of Thira,
117

Italy, Pompeii, Herculaneum and Mt. Vesu-
vius, 140
Volterra, Italy, 137

W
Walking
Austria
Salzburger Sportwelt
Amade, 51
Vienna, 51
Czech Republic, Prague,
60–61
Denmark, Stroget in
Copenhagen, 70
France
Champs Elysees in Par-
is, 81
Left Bank in Paris, 81
Montmartre in Paris, 81
Rue du Port Neuf in
Bayonne, 90
Hungary, Sopron, 124
Italy, Florence, 136
Norway, Geirangerfjord,
161
Poland, Zakopane, 169
Portugal, Evora, 179
Spain
Cape Formentor on the
Baleraric Islands,
192
Las Rambles in Barce-
lona, 189
Sweden
in general, 199
Gothenburg, 202
Switzerland
Appenzell, 215
Chur, 214
Walled towns
France
Avignon, 87
Saint Malo, 94
Greece, Rhodes, 114
Italy, Tuscany, 136–138
Portugal
Evora, 178–179
Monsaraz, 179
Obidos, 180

Spain, Minorca in the Bal-
eraric Islands, 192
Warsaw. Poland, 167–168
average temperatures and
rainfall, 243
Waterfalls
Austria
Kimmler in Zell am
Zeller, 54
Netherlands, Geirangerf-
jord, 161
Sweden, Trollhatten in Bo-
huslan, 203
Switzerland
Giessbach and Reish-
enbach Falls in
Brienz, 212
Jungfrau Region, 211
Water skiing
Switzerland
Interlaken, 211
Lugano, 213
Weather, scheduling trip, 7
Western Mediterranean Coast,
Western Turkey,
229
Western Trandanubia, Hunga-
ry, 124
Western Turkey, 220–231
Wild life, France, Camargue,
87
Windmills, Netherlands, 149
Windsurfing
Austria, Salzkammerg Ut
Region, 51
Denmark
Jutland, 74
Romo, 75
Norway, Lillehammer, 159
Switzerland, Lugano, 213
Wine
caves, Switzerland, Locar-
no, 213
cellars, Austria, 50
Wineries
France, Distillerie de la
Cote Basque in Bay-
onne, 90
Hungary
Eger, 127

Tokaj, 127
Italy, Montepulciano, 138
Portugal, Vila Nova de
Gaia in Oporto, 180
See also Vineyards
Winterthur, Switzerland, 216
Wood carving, Switzerland,
Brienz, 212
Word list
Austria, 56
Czech/Slovak, 67
Demark, 77
France, 96
Germany, 107
Greece, 118
Hungary, 129
Italy, 146
Netherlands, 153
Norway, 164
Poland, 173
Portugal, 183
Spain, 196
Sweden, 206
Switzerland, 219
Western Turkey, 231

X, Y, Z
Zakopane, Poland, 168–169
Zamosc, Poland, 170
Zealand, Denmark, 70–73
Zell am Zeller, Austria, 54
Zest, defined, 46
Zoos
Austria, Helbrunn in
Salzburg, 50
Germany
Frankfurt, 104
Salsburg, 50
Hungary, Pecs, 125
Sweden, Skansen in Stock-
holm, 200
Switzerland
Basel, 217
Zoo Dolder in Zurich,
215
Zurich, Switzerland, 215–216
average temperatures and
rainfall, 243

About the Author

Carol Mickelsen is a professional chef. She bought and restored a dilapidated but historic hotel with restaurant and bar in Half Moon Bay, California, a small town located 30 minutes south of San Francisco. The San Benito House has received rave reviews from *Gourmet Magazine* and *National Geographic Traveler* Magazine. Her oldest son now owns the business. Her youngest son has restored and operates The Wildwood, a bar/pizza place on the Klamath River Parkway in Northern California. Still doing some cooking and training of staff, Carol now greets guests in a more leisurely fashion.

Carol has traveled throughout the world. She finds budget travel fun, interesting, and easy.

About the Illustrator

Jack Tavenner is a freelance artist who lives in the Pacific Northwest. He enjoys the opportunities the region offers for camping, hiking and boating.

Video

A video "Camping Your Way Through Europe" was filmed in Switzerland that actually demonstrates many of the camping techniques described in this book. You can obtain the video by calling or writing to the publisher.